"I can't imagine any Christian not being
If you are looking for a resource that w
the issue of homosexuality with unflinchi
grace, this is a great place to start."

—from the Fc

"These pastors/authors equip us to love persons with same-sex attraction well. Born of life in the real world, their efforts are profound yet conveyed with a light touch that makes a tough subject an enjoyable read."

—Andrew Comiskey, founder/executive director,
Desert Stream/Living Waters Ministries

"*Compassion Without Compromise* seeks to be candid help on a difficult topic: the complex variations of modern sexual brokenness. You may cheer one page and jeer another. But, having heard the mind of two pastors who wrestle honestly with sexual issues every day, at least you will find help to make up your own mind."

—Dr. Todd Hunter, Anglican bishop, pastor of Holy Trinity
Anglican Church, and author of *Our Favorite Sins*

"In this timely book, Barr and Citlau offer down-to-earth advice to Christians who seek to celebrate God's intended plan for marriage, while extending compassion and hope to people trapped in homosexual lifestyles. Their proposal is filled with courage, conviction, common sense, and confidence in the power of God's gospel."

—Scott M. Manetsch, professor of church history, Trinity
Evangelical Divinity School

"Both the church and culture are being ripped apart by the homosexuality issue. Adam and Ron have given us a most important discussion of the issue that is biblical, personal, and practical. I know of no other work that encompasses all three approaches."

—Charles Simpson, author, Bible teacher,
motivational speaker, pastor

"Raw, honest, grace-filled, and boldly biblical, *Compassion Without Compromise* addresses the questions all of us are asking. If you want to talk with, walk with, and help family and friends who deal with same-sex attraction, this book provides all you need to get started."

—Kevin Harney, author of *Empowered by His Presence*
and the ORGANIC OUTREACH series, lead pastor of Shoreline
Community Church in Monterey, California

"Adam and Ron have given a gift to Christians and the church. This book will help you stay faithful to the truth of Scripture while loving people in your life who struggle with same-sex attraction.

After you read this book, you will find yourself telling others about it because of the hope and value you will draw from the wisdom contained in its pages."

—Sherry Harney, author of *Organic Outreach for Families*
and director of strategic leadership development
at Shoreline Community Church

"This book delivers exactly what the title states, 'compassion without compromise,' which is specifically what is needed today. . . . I am thankful for Adam and Ron's heart, tone, and sound interpretation of the Scriptures."

—Dan Kimball, author of *They Like Jesus but Not the Church*

"The authors ask, 'How can we be a compassionate, uncompromising witness in a culture that celebrates what the Bible censors?' And the answer they provide is as practical as it is compassionate and uncompromising."

—Dr. Samuel Logan, international director,
The World Reformed Fellowship

"With conviction and grace the authors articulate biblical teaching about the sinfulness of homosexuality. They also provide wise, loving, and practical guidelines that are profoundly useful as the church engages people in need of the light of Christ on this issue. I hope you will read the book and make it available to many in your church."

—Heath Lambert, associate professor of biblical counseling
at The Southern Baptist Theological Seminary

"I know Ron and Adam well and know firsthand that the title of this book matches who they are as disciples of Christ. I can also attest to their ability to address this hot topic with the warm grace of Christ. Christians, pastors, church leaders, and same-sex attracted persons . . . this is a must-read!"

—Bob Bouwer, senior pastor, Faith Church, Dyer, Indiana

"At last someone has written a book like *Compassion Without Compromise*! Barr and Citlau have managed to be biblically and theologically faithful, culturally astute, pastorally sensitive, and fun to read—all in just 160 pages."

—Ben Patterson, campus pastor, Westmont College,
Santa Barbara, California

"Pastors Barr and Citlau weave Scripture, theology, and personal experience to explain why homosexual practice doesn't deliver on its promise, and they give practical, compassionate counsel for dealing with the hard, personal conundrums that each of us face."

—Mike Wittmer, professor of systematic theology, Grand Rapids
Theological Seminary/Cornerstone University

COMPASSION
without
COMPROMISE

How the Gospel Frees Us to Love
Our Gay Friends Without Losing the Truth

Adam T. Barr & Ron Citlau

BETHANY HOUSE PUBLISHERS
a division of Baker Publishing Group
Minneapolis, Minnesota

Published by Bethany House Publishers
11400 Hampshire Avenue South
Bloomington, Minnesota 55438
www.bethanyhouse.com

Bethany House Publishers is a division of
Baker Publishing Group, Grand Rapids, Michigan

Printed in the United States of America

Library of Congress Cataloging-in-Publication Data
Barr, Adam T.
    Compassion without compromise : how the gospel frees us to love our gay
friends without losing the turth / Adam T. Barr and Ron Citlau.
        pages cm
    Includes bibliographical references.
    Summary: "Two pastors offer compassionate, biblical answers about homo-
sexuality and practical real world advice on how to think and talk about this
controversial issue with loved ones"— Provided by publisher.
        ISBN 978-0-7642-1240-6 (pbk. : alk. paper)
        1. Church work with gays. 2. Love—Religious aspects—Christianity.
3. Church work. 4. Homosexuality—Religious aspects—Christianity. 5. Sex—
Religious aspects—Christianity. I. Title.
BV4437.5.B37 2014
241'.664—dc23   2014018224

Cover design by LOOK Design Studio

15   16   17   18   19   20   21   9   8   7   6   5   4   3

from Adam

To my dad and mom, Randy and Sandra Barr. Thank you for showing me how to follow Jesus. Your lives are a legacy of love for the Lord, each other, and the Kingdom. I pray that same love will mark the path I leave behind.

from Ron

To Andrew Comiskey and Charlie Contreras. You were the first pastors who declared the good news of the gospel to me in my brokenness. When there was no hope, the Lord used you both to show me salvation in Jesus Christ. Your lives are witnesses of who he is and what he does. This book is, in part, the fruit of your good ministry. Thank you.

Contents

Foreword

Hardly a day goes by when we don't hear something about homosexuality. It's all over the news and all over social media. It's the subject of countless conversations, arguments, diatribes, rants, punditry, and commentary. You can't help but wonder: *Is there really anything left to say?*

Actually, there is a lot that still needs to be said. This issue is not about to fade into the background, and many of the hardest personal and pastoral questions are just beginning to surface. That's why I am delighted with this new book.

Adam and Ron are excellent pastors, good thinkers, and great friends. I've known Adam since we went to college together and I sat there jealously as he, with his long, flowing locks, played guitar and crooned in the worship team, much to the admiration of many young women. Since then we've become close friends, colleagues in ministry, and, in many ways, brothers in arms.

My friendship with Ron is not as long, but just as rich. I will never forget Ron's stirring, courageous testimony at our denomination's General Synod back in 2012. I don't think I've ever heard the gospel more poignantly and powerfully presented at such a gathering. I'm grateful for Ron's winsome, yet bold, approach to this difficult topic of sexuality. I have learned much from him.

As much as I appreciate Adam and Ron personally, that's not the reason to read this book. A much better reason is that they have teamed up to write an engaging, accessible, sensitive, uncompromising, wise, and biblical book about the most controversial issue of our day. There are other books on homosexuality—and many of them should be read alongside this one. But what makes this volume unique is the personal touch—especially Ron's story of having had gay feelings for most of his life—and the pastoral approach to the difficult questions none of us can avoid:

- Should I attend my friend's gay "wedding"?
- Should we invite our homosexual son's partner to our home for the holidays?
- How should I respond if my young child thinks he's gay?

There are dozens of questions like this in the book, each one answered with biblical insight and with good sense. I can't imagine any Christian not being helped by this book. Adam and Ron are clear about the Bible's prohibition of homosexual activity. They are informed on the latest scholarship. They are discerning when it comes to real-life application. And they are, above all, hopeful. Hopeful in the power of the gospel to save, to forgive, to restore, and to transform. If you are looking for a resource that will help you think about the issue of homosexuality with unflinching truth and with sincere grace, this is a great place to start.

—Kevin DeYoung

Introduction

We Understand. . . .
It Would Be Easy to Panic

In the next year you can bet at least one of these things will happen in your life:

- A family member will come out of the closet and expect you to be okay with it. If you are not, family members may call you unloving and judgmental.
- You'll be invited to a cousin's "wedding" . . . to someone of the same gender.
- Your elementary-age child will come home talking about bullying; the curriculum will feature a major section on the need to respect peers from LGBT* families.
- You'll show up for one of your kid's soccer games and discover that the woman who comes to every game with little Billy's mom is *not* his aunt.

* LGBT is a commonly used acronym for "Lesbian, Gay, Bisexual, Transgendered." Often, a Q will be appended to the end, indicating "Queer" or "Questioning."

- Your company human resources department will hold a session on how to build a tolerant workplace for LGBT co-workers.
- You will encounter someone who says the gospel cannot bring healing to our sexual identity or orientation.
- You'll have to share a bathroom with someone of the opposite gender who self-identifies as your own.
- You'll have a conversation with your college-age child and learn she thinks your view on homosexuality is bigoted, a twenty-first-century version of 1960s racism.
- You will read about a nationally recognized church leader endorsing the idea of same-sex marriage.

Are you ready?

Are you ready to answer the tough questions your friends are asking you about your beliefs? Are you ready to reply to the wedding invitation from your gay cousin? Are you ready to deal with your daughter's new friend, her two mommies, and the invitation for a sleepover? Are you ready to show someone that you can really, truly love people *and* still believe that sin is sin?

Are you ready, or are you panicking?

If you are reading this book, chances are you would answer in the affirmative if someone asked you, "Is homosexual behavior a sin?" But consider three follow-up questions:

First, why do you believe this? Is it simply because "that's how I was raised"? Is it because you find "those people" kind of "gross" and "weird"? Reality check: If our convictions are that shallow, then how can we respond with Christlike compassion to people Jesus died to save? How will you be a real witness to the gospel? How will your faith survive when one of "those people" turns out to be someone you know and love? People gripped by the gospel are able to reach out to *anyone* in a way that balances truth and love.

Second, have you taken time to really explore what the Bible teaches about sexuality? You might (correctly) believe that Scripture says homosexual activity is a sin, but are you prepared to help someone else see that? Are you ready to defend your beliefs when someone persuasively argues that the Bible does not really condemn loving, committed same-sex relationships? Simply responding, "It's what I've always believed" will not help you be a faithful witness. It will not help you when smart people ask hard questions.

Third, if your convictions on this issue are not well founded on rock-solid truth, do you really think they will stand the test of a hard storm? Jesus said that someone who hears his Word and obeys it is like a person who has built his house on a solid rock. The rain comes, the wind rages, but the house stands. If our stated convictions are not undergirded by solid foundations, they can be quickly swept aside. On this issue, Christians who faithfully speak the truth will increasingly stand in the minority. In the last decade alone, our culture has experienced a revolution of thought when it comes to homosexuality. The pressure to conform will be intense.

Are you ready?

Or are you panicking?

Trust Us. . . . You Don't Need to Panic

Why would two thirty-something guys write a book about homosexuality? Do we have an ax to grind or a hobbyhorse to ride? Are we just modern-day Pharisees who want to pick on one sin? What motivates us, and why are we qualified to answer your questions?

One simple answer: We are pastors. That means we routinely sit with real people and hear their stories. We have listened to teenage boys who wonder why they're attracted to other boys and are compulsively driven to view homosexual pornography. We have prayed with parents who just learned their firstborn son is living with another man. We have church members come up and ask questions like, "So, is it wrong for me to tell my nephew that he can't bring his boyfriend to Thanksgiving dinner?"

Each week we write sermons, care for church members, lead meetings, teach classes, organize ministries, and write devotionals. Our pastoral lives are full and exciting. And one of the greatest blessings of our work is getting to see how what we teach impacts real people every single day.

Additionally, each of us is a husband and a dad. We love our wives and children. Each of us has been married to his wife for more than a decade. Each of us has four sons. We coach soccer, go to awards ceremonies, attend parent-teacher meetings. . . . You get the picture. Life is full, demanding, and very satisfying. And we both wonder, *What will happen as our own kids grow up in a world that has increasingly decided to celebrate what the Bible censors? How can we, as pastors and fathers, help our kids navigate this new world?*

We think it's time for a book that will help real people, living in the real world, to give real answers. That is what motivates us to write. And that is why we think we have something to say that will help you.

While our motives are very similar, the stories that shaped them are very different. In the coming chapters, we are going to be exploring some issues that cut close to the heart. So before we do that, we thought we should share our stories with you.

Ron: A Story of Restoration

I am a Christian, husband, father of four boys, and pastor, and I have had gay feelings for most of my life. These feelings have shamed me, delighted me, hurt me, and confused me. As a teenager, I grew up in church and did not know what to do with these impulses. Because of great fear, I never shared the sexual chaos that I was experiencing with anyone in the church I attended. As an adolescent, in the isolation of that chaos, an adult man befriended me and sexually abused me.

From there, my life spiraled out of control—marked by intense drug use and promiscuous same-sex sexual behavior. This was my teenage and early adult life. Though I had many partners, I was all alone. It was hard. It was painful, and it was the darkest time of my life. It was in this horrible place that I met Jesus. Seventeen years ago, Jesus pursued me and found me, and my life is radically different because of him. I love the life that Jesus has given me!

When Adam and I first began collaborating on this book, I wasn't sure I wanted my sex life in print. God has done an amazing work in my life; there is a part of me that just wants to live out my freedom and wholeness in private. But as I prayed and considered the idea, I realized that this book needed to be written.

This book needed to be written because the gospel is amazing news for the sexual sinner. I have experienced the bondage of sexual sin. I did not find freedom, fulfillment, and wholeness in the exploration of my gay desire, far from it. All I experienced was brokenness and lostness. When I pursued homosexuality, the result was a life decimated by sin.

Thank God, there is good news! In 1997, I said yes to Jesus and began attending a local church in Southern California, where I lived. This church knew how to walk with me; it had experience in helping people find Jesus in their brokenness. They understood that the gospel of Jesus was good news to the sexual sinner. Over the next five years, I grew as a follower of Jesus, and slowly God began to bring gospel transformation to my life.

This transformation began for me with God's sweet love that accepted me as I was—sinful, broken, and confused. Transformation continued as I repented of the many sins I had committed sexually. Then, as I accepted his love and experienced his forgiveness, transformation commanded and created sexual purity. Out of love, repentance, and purity, I began to see the reordering of my sexual desire.

As I look back over the last seventeen years, I see that Jesus and his gospel have profoundly transformed me as a sexual person. I am a different man than I used to be. This book needs to be written because the gospel for the sexual sinner is being reduced, marginalized, and treated like something to forget whenever possible or apologize for whenever required. There is good news! And Adam and I want to tell it.

Christ's gospel is the hope for the sexual sinner. Jesus can and does do extraordinary things for anyone who would put his or her trust in him. Whether it is hope-filled celibacy or profound sexual transformation, Jesus is in the business of changing lives! I have had the great honor of walking with many men and women who are honoring Christ in their sexuality and who have been radically touched by the gospel. What I have experienced personally and have seen in the church is not unique or peculiar. I believe this is the good news of Jesus, and I am writing this book to share it.

Adam: A Love for the Church

"I want you to break into groups of three to five people," my professor instructed. "You are church members who have gathered to discuss a sensitive issue. Here is the topic: How should our church respond to the news that one of our elders' children is gay? Should we condemn this son of the church as sinful, or should we welcome him as one of God's children?"

The year was 1994. I was a sophomore taking a summer intensive course at my smallish, well-respected Christian college. The class was called Christian Love. The professor was a local pastor and active leader in my denomination, the Reformed Church in America. In the discussion that followed, I realized very soon that my grasp of the topic was weak.

I can still remember the chaos and confusion shooting through the debate that day. It did not take long for people to draw up sides. In just a few moments, fellow students stopped trying to act out their parts. The illusion that we were grown-up church leaders soon dissolved and we were speaking like young adults with strong opinions, little information, and lots of passion.

When the bell rang at the end of class, I walked away with a few distinct impressions. I knew I would need to get a better grip on the Bible's teaching about human sexuality. I realized that simple responses to homosexuality like "Love the sinner, hate the sin" really were *not* going to cut it in the years ahead. I wondered how in the world the gospel would be good news in a culture where conversations would increasingly look and sound like the "dialogue" that took place in that classroom.

Of the many convictions that pressed their way into my thinking after class, one stood out sharp and clear: *The church is going to be divided on this issue.* It seemed certain that some Christian thinkers would embrace our culture's trend toward open and affirming acceptance of homosexuality. Others would cling to the truth but completely disengage from our culture, slipping into irrelevance. *Was there another way?*

That question was important to me for many reasons. I grew up in a ministry family. My dad served more than thirty years as a pastor. Unlike many PKs (pastor's kids) I actually grew up with a deep love for the church. The thought that Christians would be divided on this issue grieved me deeply. Still more, I wrestled with real frustration and sadness, knowing that in one way or another, people were going to be led astray.

Even as a nineteen-year-old college student I saw one thing clearly: This was much more than an academic discussion. Entire families would be fractured or fixed depending on how the church addressed this issue. People would experience deep healing or dark despair. God's people would be moving closer to him in obedience or wandering further away from him in rebellion. Ultimately, people's eternal destinies would be impacted by the answers to the questions we asked that day in a college class called Christian Love.

Why am I writing this book? Because the years since that class have only strengthened my conviction that this issue has the potential to divide God's people. Actually, I would put the matter a little more starkly: This issue is already dividing God's people. And when the church does not preach the gospel with a unified voice, the only light of the world is diminished. I write this book believing that God wants his people to be united around the truth on this issue. Only then can we reach out in love, holding forth the gospel as the only hope for sinners like us. And only then can we be free.

We Need Help!

This book needed to be written because the church needs help with how it addresses homosexuality. For the last three decades, evangelicals have tried to stand against the tide. We have tried to turn it back and "take back" our country. It is time to realize something: The ship has sailed. The question is no longer *Can we win the culture wars?* Rather, it is *How can we be a compassionate, uncompromising witness in a culture that celebrates what the Bible censors?*

We both serve in a denomination that is being ripped apart by this issue. On one side stand churches that embrace homosexuals, tell them God created them gay, and emphasize that the church ought to welcome them, marry them, and place them in leadership. On another side are churches that see homosexual activity as sin but can come across as insular—sometimes seeming bigoted or even hostile toward people who identify as gay or lesbian. In the middle, many well-intentioned Christians are afraid of hurting their gay friends and family. They would rather live as if homosexuality is not a critical issue.

As pastors, we want to help Christians navigate the new cultural landscape that is emerging. In the coming decade, we will discover that debate is not on the menu. We will be encouraged to choose between two equally unattractive alternatives: Either "join the team" that is open and affirming or sit on the sidelines, be labeled a bigot, and shut up. It is already happening.

College and high school students are being exposed to a number of key undermining claims aimed at overturning a traditional view of human sexuality. The claims of science are being leveraged against traditional morality. The claims of revisionist biblical interpreters are being employed to persuade the faithful.

An "open and affirming" message is being asserted everywhere, not just in Hollywood. As you read this book, students at colleges that once trained missionaries and pastors are being encouraged by their professors to change their views of human sexuality and biblical norms. They are attending lectures, workshops, and discussion groups meant to persuade them to reframe the Bible's message. Not surprisingly, it's not hard to convince them to do that. When students have never really heard a clear presentation of biblical truth on the issue, a moderately sophisticated presentation of unbiblical teaching will go down easy.

So how can we show compassion without compromise in a world like this?

We hope this book will help you begin answering that question. It is not exhaustive, but everything you read here is like a door that will lead you to further insight on the issue. We want to be pastorally helpful. We want to answer the questions that you are facing as a follower of Jesus in a clear, simple, and biblical way. In the last decade, brilliant authors have penned excellent theological and therapeutic works to address the issue of homosexuality. We will list some of them in our endnotes and a list of recommended resources at the back of the book. At the same time, we believe the church needs an accessible resource that gives clear biblical teaching, answers tough questions, and shares personal stories. This kind of book will help Christians in our changing world find balanced ways to respond to the issue of homosexuality.

This is why we are writing this book. We want to help you hold out the true hope of the gospel to *everyone*. That hope is not simple affirmation. It is much more than mere tolerance. Our hope begins with the message that we all need God's forgiveness and joyfully proclaims that Jesus has made a way. It is a message of freedom. We are called to bring that message to the world.

And the world is waiting.

1

Something Beautiful

Why did God make sex?

Birds, Bees, and a Medical Dictionary

I (Adam) was in first grade. Her name was Kirsten. We were classmates at the same Christian school, and her parents had dropped her off at my house for a play date. That is what I remember.

Looking back, I realize I was somewhere between Stage 1 and Stage 2. Just so we are all on the same page, let me explain what I mean by these stages. At the ripe old age of thirty-nine, I have come to the entirely unscientific conviction that boys generally move through three stages when it comes to girls.

At Stage 1, boys register very little distinction between themselves and the opposite sex. At this stage, boys will play sports with girls, knocking them down and expecting them to react just like the boys would. As a father of four boys myself, I can testify: We should not hold this kind of behavior against them. They are not responsible, because, frankly, they just don't know any better! Their female peers are only distinguished by longer hair and a passion for things like glittery pink-maned ponies.

At Stage 2, boys have determined that all girls have *cooties* (archaic word for lice). Girls, they reason, are weird, gross, and like to play with dolls! In the mind of a Stage 2 boy, girls are like canned asparagus (to be avoided). At this stage, we see a radical separation of the sexes. Generally speaking, girls are fine with this arrangement, thank you very much.

Stage 3 comes at different times for different boys. The more mature, "with it" guys get there much sooner. At this stage, boys suddenly realize that girls are not only different, but totally awesome. Girls become an obsession for boys at this point. At sleepovers, boys talk about which girl is "hot" and which girl is not. They start becoming concerned with whether or not they are in the A-crowd or B-crowd. Boys no longer need to be reminded to take a shower or use deodorant. In fact, most social considerations revolve around whether the presenting options will help them get a girl to notice them or not.

I am not sure whether these stages still apply. After all, the world has changed a lot since I was a boy in the early 1980s. But for many boys back then, these were the essential periods of development. My four sons are still growing, but so far seem to be tracking right along this developmental path.

As I said, I was somewhere between Stage 1 and Stage 2. When I thought about it hard enough, I decided it was weird for Kirsten to be at my house, but as we got lost in a game of hide-and-seek or basketball she was "just one of the guys."

At a certain point in the day, Kirsten and I decided we needed to find my mom, so we searched the house. But Mom was nowhere to be found. Next we looked for Dad. He was AWOL too. In reality, we probably checked a room or two, then gave up.

Kirsten and I found ourselves back out in the yard, looking up at my house. I can still remember sheepishly muttering something like, "This just isn't like Mom and Dad. They're usually much more responsible than this. I wonder where they are." At that point, Kirsten said something that changed my world forever.

"Maybe they're upstairs . . . in their room . . . without any clothes on," she suggested in a tone that blended insider knowledge and nervous hilarity in equal measure.

I was shocked and scandalized. Looking at her with disbelief, I replied, "I don't think my parents would do that sort of thing."

Man, was I wrong.

I learned just *how* wrong a few months later. It started with an innocent question for my mom and ended with our sitting down, a medical dictionary on her lap, and questions rushing through my mind at light speed.

Long story short, we had "the talk." My mother explained the meaning and mechanics of menstruation. She reviewed the ins and outs of copulation, and then she dropped the big one: This is how babies are made! She patiently answered my questions, one by one—and being an insatiably curious kid, there were many. I simultaneously felt grown-up, naïve, curious, and grossed out beyond description. Finally, Mom asked, "Do you have any other questions?"

"Yes," I replied, "Why in the *world* would you want to do that?"

Mom paused and thought for a moment. "Well . . . because that is how husbands and wives show their love. And because that is how *you* were born. And, well, because it's fun."

Looking back, I cannot imagine Mom giving a better answer. In that moment she affirmed some important things. First, she told me that sex was a good, God-given gift, not some unspeakable mystery to be explored in the back seat of a car. Second, she told me that sex was something for marriage. Third, she presented a child-appropriate understanding that our sexuality is meant to be a source of pleasure and joy.

Thanks, Mom.

When we look at Scripture, we find that a lot of the elements of my mom's response are contained in God's view of sexuality. That is important to note, because God designed sex in the first place. As such, he knows better than anyone exactly why we have it and exactly where and how we should enjoy it.

Something we should clarify up front: We believe that God has given us his perspective on a whole host of things. The Bible, we believe, is God's Word. When we open the Scriptures, we are encountering much more than human thoughts about God. In fact, we are encountering God's thoughts. Of course, God used human beings to write the Bible. He enlisted shepherds, priests, poets, physicians, and fishermen. Over 2,000 years ago, he used urban sophisticates and rural hicks. But in all the various voices and different styles, one voice speaks clearly in every word: the voice of the God who created us.

Maybe you believe this and maybe you don't. Whatever your personal convictions on the matter, we thought it would be important for you to understand how we are approaching the Bible. We believe there are many good reasons to read Scripture this way. If you would like to learn a little more about why this issue is important, check out the appendix: "The Watershed." For now, understand that we are going to do our level best to describe what Scripture says about human sexuality. Our perspective on homosexuality is shaped by an earnest effort to understand God's perspective. And the Bible is where we turn for that.

That said, let's look at what the Bible says about sex. The best possible place for us to turn is to the very beginning, where it was created.

Life in the Garden

Now the LORD God had formed out of the ground all the beasts of the field and all the birds of the air. He brought them to the man to see what he would name them; and whatever the man called each living creature, that was its name. So the man gave names to all the livestock, the birds of the air and all the beasts of the field.

But for Adam no suitable helper was found. So the LORD God caused the man to fall into a deep sleep; and while he was sleeping, he took one of the man's ribs and closed up the place with flesh. Then the LORD God made a woman from the rib he had taken out of the man, and he brought her to the man.

The man said,

"This is now bone of my bones
and flesh of my flesh;
she shall be called 'woman,'
for she was taken out of man."

For this reason a man will leave his father and mother and be united to his wife, and they will become one flesh.

The man and his wife were both naked, and they felt no shame.

Genesis 2:19–25 (NIV 1984)

In this opening section of the Bible, we are given a glimpse of how God designed the DNA of human relationships, an insight into what it means to be a person. Philosophers gaze from their navels to the heavens and beyond. Psychologists set out on the chaotic oceans of the id. Physicians run EKG tests and administer physical well-being. In other words, a lot of smart individuals try to help us understand what it means to be healthy, happy people. Here in Genesis, we discover a snapshot of what human flourishing really looks like from the One who created it, giving us the essential components of meaningful existence. The Designer of life deserves our attention.

The first thing to notice is that everybody needs somebody. Humans are not made to be alone. Just a few verses before, we read that of all the great things he had made only one was "not good." God decided that it was not good for man to be all by himself. That is why verses 19 through 20 are all about Adam meeting the animals. Each one is brought to him. He gives it a name (exercising a godlike authority). But none of them is a fit partner for Adam.

A partner in what? Basically a partner in living. God wants Adam to have a helper, a companion to walk through life with as he seeks to fulfill his purpose. We could turn back to Genesis 1 and realize what that purpose is: to bear God's image, living as God's representative on earth, loving as God does, thinking as God does, and in a very small way, representing the power of God. God wanted Adam to have help with that.

The helper would need to be like Adam but different from him. In some miraculous way that we never would have imagined, God wanted a same-but-different kind of creature to be Adam's companion. They would have to share an essential bond, not like two peas in a pod, but more complementary, like a lock and key, biceps and triceps, or a left pedal and right pedal . . . you get the picture.

And so God put Adam to sleep, took part of him, and made Eve. Don't ask us how that worked. The actual biological process of the event is not what is most important here. What matters is that God was hands on the whole way. He handcrafted Eve from Adam's rib, just as he molded Adam from the dust of the ground.

The moment Adam saw Eve, everything made sense. Like a puzzle the moment the pieces come together, it was clear that no other arrangement could have worked! Like Adam, Eve was a moving, thinking, physical-spiritual creature made in God's image. Just like the rib God took to make her, Eve could be at Adam's side, a partner in the task of making God's garden grow.

In essential and obvious ways, she was different too. Let's get this out of the way: Eve had a vagina. Adam had a penis. We weren't there, but we figure that was one of the things Adam noticed right away. But this surface distinction in biological arrangement was reflective of a deeper difference in purpose. Actually, we could put a finer point on this. This distinction in appearance was reflective of a sameness-difference in purpose. Let us explain.

Reading the creation account, one thing we see is that God wrote a *principle of reproduction* into all living things. Living things are meant to make more living things (see Genesis 1:11–13, 20–25). Life makes life. Our bet is that God is letting us, in some small way, reflect his eternal life, his never-ending reservoir of energy, power, and goodness—like a river of life with no beginning or end. We creatures are allowed to physically represent that spiritual reality by reproducing life.

Adam and Eve were designed to manifest that principle together, but in very different ways. Adam would give. Eve would receive. Like a farmer, Adam would plant seed. Like the verdant garden, Eve would nurture life within herself. Of course, it was even more complex than this. It was not as if Adam had all the seed. We learn in Biology 101 that even at the smallest microscopic level, there is a reproductive partnership expressed in chromosomes coming together like lock and key, laying down genetic patterns and unleashing DNA. From the very obvious way the male and female anatomy fit together to the subtle pairing of genetic information, Adam and Eve were designed for reproduction.

This story does not exist simply to describe how Adam and Eve met, fell in love, and enjoyed life without tan lines. Genesis 2:24 (NIV 1984) helps us understand the theological significance of this event: *"For this reason a man will leave his father and mother and be united to his wife, and they will become one flesh.*" Another way to put this is: The reason God made man and woman with this same-but-different design is so that they could experience and enjoy an intimate, lifelong union. So in addition to the *principle of reproduction*, we also see the *principle of union* built into God's purposes for Adam and Eve. They were designed by God to be joined together as "one flesh" not only in the physical act of marriage but also in a lifelong covenant.

The one-flesh union of verse 24 does more than illustrate principles. It also allows us to live as creatures that reflect God's glory. For a moment, consider the Trinity. This mystery at the heart of our Christian faith proclaims that God is three-in-one. God is one God. God is three persons. As stated in the Athanasian Creed, not one person is less or more God than another. These persons are joined in a union that can only be described as oneness, yet distinguished in a way that must be categorized as three. Some theologians have likened this union-communion of God to a dance or a family (the Greek word is *perichoresis*). In an amazing, creaturely way, the husband-wife one-flesh union reflects the light of God's eternal community, the Trinity.

In this story and throughout Scripture, human life is not viewed as an end in itself. We are not merely creatures who are born, try to find meaning to life, and then die. In fact, we are beings designed by God and created with purpose. As unique, physical-spiritual creatures, we are designed to find joy and meaning as we live out this purpose in our everyday lives. Even more important, when we live in harmony with God's design, we give him glory. In fact, it is precisely through our joy in his plan that God is most glorified.

When We Leave the Garden . . .

But the serpent said to the woman, "You will not surely die. For God knows that when you eat of it your eyes will be opened, and you will be like God, knowing good and evil." So when the woman saw that the tree was good for food, and that it was a delight to the eyes, and that the tree was to be desired to make one wise, she took of its fruit and ate, and she also gave some to her husband who was with her, and he ate. Then the eyes of both were opened, and they knew that they were naked. And they sewed fig leaves together and made themselves loincloths.

Genesis 3:4–7

We often think of sin as simply breaking the rules. Sin certainly has a rule-breaking component. Let's face it, though, we tend to think of rules as something on paper, in books. For a lot of us, rules are made to be broken. Many people find it difficult to feel personally connected to rules. But sin is personal. Sin has everything to do with relationship. Sin is more than ignoring a dictate in God's *Personnel Manual for Human Life.*

Throughout Scripture, sin is portrayed as an effort to live as if God doesn't matter. In fact, it is portrayed as an effort to be like little gods. Sin, biblically speaking, is turning one's back on God, the God who wants us to live in a face-to-face relationship with him.

Just as Genesis 2 gives us the original design plan for human sexuality, Genesis 3 takes us back to the very first crime scene. What do we find? A man and woman, trying to live in God's world while ignoring his Word. They are, of course, breaking the rules. God gave them a clear command, "Don't eat from the tree of the knowledge of good and evil" (see Genesis 2:17). They disobeyed.

But it was not simply the rules they were rejecting. It was the right of the Creator to give them the rules. Even more, they were rejecting the wisdom of the Creator who designed them. (And that was a really dumb thing to do.)

Think for a moment: Why are there rules? Imagine playing baseball with an umpire who constantly changed the strike zone.

Imagine that this ump simply ignored the "tie goes to the runner" rule or jettisoned the "four balls equal a walk" rule. If the ump threw out enough of the rules, eventually there would be no game. There would just be a bunch of guys in funny pants trying to hit leather-wrapped balls of string with sticks! The rules are not the point of the game, but without the rules, there is no game.

God's command was given to Adam and Eve so they could understand the design plan of creation. He knew that if they stepped outside that divine plan, they would be doing much more than breaking a rule, they would be trying to live in a world that doesn't exist. We understand this when it comes to things like gravity.

As a kid, I (Adam) was obsessed with defying gravity. My first foray into the business of flying was simple: I picked up one leg and then picked up the second one very quickly, hoping to hold myself up in the air. Realizing my first plan was creative but unrealistic, I graduated from that to a plastic shopping bag, reasoning it would work like a parachute. When that failed, I assumed that I simply needed more height so there would be more time for the air to fill the bag. Eventually, I found myself on top of the garage, counting to three, and jumping.

It didn't work.

Are you surprised?

Of course not.

Just as we cannot simply change the reality of gravity on a whim, the laws of morality are much more than arbitrary lines in a heavenly rule book. They are reflections of the world as it was created. God designed a world with physical rules like gravity and wove throughout this universe a design for human flourishing reflected and described in the moral law. So when Adam and Eve decided to ignore God's word, they were doing something as silly as jumping from a garage roof with a plastic shopping bag to slow their descent.

Not surprisingly, they fell. It is the saddest story ever. Like a central theme in a great symphony, this simple story is played out again and again in daily human life. Every time we assert our will to power, our plan for existence—as if God's plan doesn't count—then we, like Adam and Eve, are falling; we are walking the road that leads out of the garden and into the desert.

As we look through the Bible to see what it has to say about homosexuality, we will need to keep something in mind: For the biblical authors, questions of sexual ethics were not framed in terms of "Does some behavior cross an arbitrary line?" The real question was "Does this behavior honor the Creator's plan for human sexuality?" If the answer was no, then the behavior was censored, precisely because it would lead people out of the garden of God's blessing and into the desert.

Of course, you do not need us to tell you that there are all kinds of sexual practices alive and well in our culture. In the world and in the church, people are throwing the Creator's good plan for sex and marriage out the window. We are quickly becoming a society that denies reality; we are jumping out into the moral firmament with gravity defiance on our minds.

As we write, even people who claim to follow Jesus are jumping feetfirst into the "hookup culture" so prevalent in society. Frightening numbers of Christians struggle with porn addiction. Heterosexual marriages are breaking apart at an alarming rate outside *and* inside the Christian community. Some would argue that these problems are at least as important to the health of the church as the behavior of two same-sex adults. We could agree—sort of.

One reason we need to call out this issue and revisit the Bible's message is because—unlike other sexual sins plaguing our churches and culture—we are being told that homosexuality *isn't* a sin. We are being told that we can live in God's world without his Word. *And that is serious.* There is no way back into the garden but through the gate that God himself opens. Whatever ethical question we're asking, if the answer we give contradicts God's revealed Word his blessings will never flow our way. Obedience to his will opens up the possibility of renewal, redemption, and abundant life in the world he has created.

Note: Each of our chapters will have a short "takeaway" section. This is designed to help you grasp the main point of the chapter and tuck it away for later reference.

God, the Creator of humanity, wants us to experience joy and life in our sexuality. But unless we live in his world according to his Word, we are going to experience tragedy—like Adam and Eve's expulsion from the garden of Eden. From the beginning, God created sexual intimacy for one man and one woman, in a lifetime covenant that reflects his glory.

2

Two-Faced

How can a bunch of hypocrites cast the first stone?

A few years ago, we had a brilliant, creative young woman in our community who struggled with homosexuality. My wife, Amy, and I (Ron) saw the great potential in her and were honored to have her actively involved in our church. She was so gifted. Like everyone else, she was called to walk out her salvation in truth and grace. For a few years, "Susan" decided to deal with her same-sex struggle from a conservative evangelical perspective. She was faithful—went to both support groups and Bible studies, sought to be honest about what was going on, and from my viewpoint, began to grow and bear the fruit of discipleship.

But for a variety of reasons, she decided that she wanted to embrace her gay identity. So she did. She left our community and began to live the life she wanted to live. We still stayed connected on Facebook. Over the next several months she began to post some eye-opening statements about the church where I was a pastor. From her point of view, she saw the church as judgmental, homophobic, and filled with people who had their own sin problems and were not willing to be gracious to others. "Who are they to judge me?" she wrote. Shouldn't we keep quiet and get our own lives in order?

It would be easy to dismiss her concerns and say that her criticism didn't matter. After all, she was bitter. No need to listen. But she is a part of a growing chorus of voices, inside and outside the church, asking important questions, questions that need to be answered.

Susan is right. The church *is* filled with people who disobey Scripture. Sexual sins abound in the Christian community—infidelity, divorce, pornography, and cohabitation, to name a few. The church has a serious sin problem. We admit it. We apologize for it. This fact doesn't change the truth that God has a plan for sexuality. What follows is an attempt to explain why the church can take a stand on the issue of homosexuality. It is by no means exhaustive, but it is a good place to start.

We Are All Struggling

For several years, I (Ron) was the pastor of the twenty-something group at a very large church in the Chicago area. Whether those who came to this group were committed to Jesus or not, many if not most had serious struggles with sin, much of it sexual. The use of pornography was rampant, and sexual intimacy among unmarried young adults was seen as something to be expected, even among Christians. Of course these young adults knew the biblical demands for purity and chastity, but their lives didn't reflect the truth they knew in their heads. These few hundred young adults are a microcosm of an undeniable reality: The church is full of sinners. Does this mean we should be silent because we are men and women with serious areas of sin and darkness in our lives?

No. The truth still stands, even if we fail to live up to it. C. S. Lewis helps us here. He writes,

> We must, therefore, not be surprised if we find among the Christians some people who are still nasty. There is even, when you come to think it over, a reason why nasty people might be expected to turn to Christ in greater numbers than nice ones. That was what people objected to about Christ during His life on earth: He seemed to attract "such awful people."[1]

Just because we can find sinners and hypocrites in any church—and if we're honest, this describes every one of us—it does not mean that the church is without a voice. In fact, all it means is that we need to be more honest about the fact that we too have missed the mark. This doesn't excuse us, nor does it excuse the same-sex struggler. It reveals the need we each have for Jesus.

Maybe humility is what our standing for truth needs. Donald Miller, in his book *Blue Like Jazz*, talks about how he and his friends set up a confessional booth, as *Leadership Journal* put it, "at Reed College in Portland, Oregon, a decidedly secular and highly intellectual place that *Princeton Review* named 'the college where students are most likely to ignore God.'"[2] Instead of getting the pagans to confess their sins, the Christians went about sharing the ways that they and many others had missed the mark of their Master, Jesus Christ.

This is the right posture to take in a world that is looking for ways to despise and disregard Christians. We need to be honest about our failures and sins. None of us lives up to the standards our faith demands. Maybe this posture of humility will gain the gospel a fresh hearing. But this honest humility does not mean there are no standards. Instead, it reveals our deep need for mercy, the kind of mercy Lewis says is so attractive to "such awful people." Jesus is our only hope. And yes, he is the only hope for the same-sex struggler as well.

That Being Said . . .

I (Ron) am a father of four boys. What is so interesting about parenting is that these boys act just like me. It isn't so much what I say that matters. It is who I am that is shaping them. This is a sobering reality. I can tell them to be respectful to one another all day long, but if I don't show respect for them and my wife, my word doesn't mean much. Of course there is grace. But I want my children to grow up to be godly men, as much as I have a say in it.

What is true at home is true in the world. Our behavior speaks at least as loudly as our words. Jesus is clear: "If you love me, you will keep my commandments" (John 14:15). There is a laxity in Christian morality today that is troubling. When Christians are confronted, they use the cover of grace as an excuse for immorality. The LGBT community has a point. Why should they take what Jesus says seriously if his followers don't? We need to take seriously the demands of Jesus. We need to decide to actually follow him. What a great refutation it would be to a world that considers Christians hypocrites if we actually began to look like Jesus.

Scripture Is Our Guide

Even a cursory reading of Scripture will tell you that homosexual activity is considered sin (the question is covered in depth in chapters 4 and 5). For the most part, both liberal and conservative theologians agree on this. No one can convincingly conclude that Paul was in favor of homosexual activity. Few scholars would argue that Jesus, a first-century Jew, would be a proponent of same-sex marriage. It is a preposterous notion. But what many liberal theologians will debate is how much weight we should give Paul and Jesus and the Scriptures that record their teachings. Some say Jesus and Paul were products of their times and must be reinterpreted by what we know now. (See what Dan Via, one of the best theologians from a liberal perspective, has to say in Robert A. J. Gagnon, *Homosexuality and the Bible: Two Views*.)

Any serious follower of Jesus must decide how he or she views the Bible: Is it the Word of God? Is it infallible? Inerrant? A guide for life? And if so, what do these words actually mean?

The traditional view of Scripture is that it is the essential guide for truth and reality. Culture does not get to reinterpret it. Instead, the Bible is the ultimate discerner in all matters of life. It is given to us by God so that his people might know how to live life well. Kevin DeYoung writes,

> Until fairly recently, Christians of every tradition have assumed the complete trustworthiness and comprehensive truthfulness of Scripture. Holding to the highest view of inspiration—as originated with God himself—was not the invention of any tradition, theologian, or school. It was simply part of what it meant to be a Christian.[3]

Scripture is the highest authority in all matters of life for the human person. Its claim is to be the surest knowledge available for life. The apostle Paul brings this point home:

> All Scripture is breathed out by God and profitable for teaching, for reproof, for correction, and for training in righteousness, that the man of God may be complete, equipped for every good work.
>
> 2 Timothy 3:16–17

In the Scriptures, we can find God's will for human sexuality. To follow Jesus is to take his view on sexuality, marriage, and relationships. His point of view is not outdated. It is simply right. No one gets to come to the Scriptures with his or her own demands. Scripture has its demands. As it relates to sexuality, Scripture is crystal clear.

Its view on sexuality, marriage, and purity are not popular today. But we can't change Scripture because it isn't culturally palatable. We are the ones who need to change.

Knowledge Matters

Imagine that you wanted to jump out of a plane with a parachute. The first thing you would do is research parachutes, get some practical training, and find places where you could do this activity safely. Once you felt confident that you knew what you were getting into, you would probably make a phone call and sign up to act on what you decided was safe to do. This is a step based on belief. You haven't done anything yet, but you have the information, it seems reliable, and you are prepared to act on it. Once you go through your training and your instructors think you are ready, you will need to get in the airplane, wait for it to reach the proper altitude, open the door, and do the insane thing: jump. This is called faith. You have gathered the information, done the training, and now you are relying on what you have learned should happen. Once you jump, there is no turning back. If all goes well, the parachute will open and you will land safely. The experience will be like none other.

Today, we need people who will take the truth of Scripture concerning homosexuality and apply it to their lives. We need people not only with faith but also with knowledge.

Plenty of people have an opinion about homosexuality, informed or not. And we have good people who have faith in the Scriptures, who believe what it says concerning sexuality. This is important. But the people we need to hear from are men and women who struggle with same-sex attraction and who also have knowledge of what God can do in and through the person of Jesus Christ.

One of the primary reasons that I am writing this book with Adam is that I have knowledge of the gospel and what it can do for the sexual sinner. This is not just abstract theory for me. I have learned what it means to live with such a struggle and have found Jesus' life and mercy in the midst of it. I have knowledge of the goodness of living in the demands, constraints, and liberty of Christian sexuality. Such people with knowledge can stand in the public square and with compassion, integrity, and conviction declare the good news of the gospel. They aren't only sharing an opinion but also reality. They are sharing knowledge of the way things should be and can be.

Just Because It's Difficult

I have been walking out my salvation for close to two decades, and I cannot tell you how many same-sex strugglers have simply quit fighting and decided to embrace their gay identity. For many, this seems to make the case that Christianity has very little to say to those struggling with their sexual identity. This simply is not true.

Dallas Willard writes, "To undertake the disciplines was to take our activities—our lives—seriously and to suppose that the following of Christ was at least as big a challenge as playing the violin or jogging."[4] I think many men and women who struggle with same-sex attraction conclude that because the struggle is so hard, God must not want them to continue resisting. Such a conclusion is about as far from historical Christianity as one can get. C. S. Lewis helps us see what Christ is up to:

> The Christian way is different: harder, and easier. Christ says, "Give me All. I don't want so much of your time and so much of

your money and so much of your work: I want You. I have not come to torment your natural self, but to kill it. No half-measures are any good. I don't want to cut off a branch here and a branch there, I want to have the whole tree down. I don't want to drill the tooth, or crown it, or stop it, but to have it out. Hand over the whole natural self, all the desires which you think innocent as well as the ones you think wicked—the whole outfit. I will give you a new self instead. In fact, I will give you Myself: my own will shall become yours."[5]

It is hard to walk with the reality of the same-sex struggle. But that is exactly the point. Each person who seeks to follow Jesus, if they actually try to do it, will find it quite hard. The demands of the gospel are harsh: Anyone who would follow him must die to self—that is, to their self-desire, their self-will. So the notion that the gospel doesn't work for those who struggle with same-sex desire is simply not true. There are countless examples of men and women who have managed their brokenness and had great victory, even in the midst of great struggle and pain. Truth be told, it doesn't work if you're not willing to take the medicine. The medicine is strong. The cure is costly. But make no mistake: What Christ did on the cross *works* for every man and woman—no matter the ailment.

Conclusion

The church is made up of sinners. But this does not make the church's voice invalid. The church must engage the culture with humility and truth. Certainly a huge cultural shift is occurring in the world today. The church's voice on a traditional view of sexuality is being shut out for what many assert to be a more palatable reality. This is unfortunate, but it is true. The church must return to its biblical foundations, unafraid to proclaim the good, hard news of the gospel. What we share from Scripture isn't a bunch of opinions. It is God's Word to us. And as those with same-sex struggles—who have met Jesus in their brokenness—proclaim what Jesus has done for them, the church will find that it does have a voice in the public square.

Takeaway

In this chapter, we admitted a tough truth: The church is full of people who disobey Scripture. Sexual sins abound in the Christian community—infidelity, divorce, pornography, and cohabitation, to name a few. The church has a serious sin problem. What binds us together is not our moral perfection but our common confession. We must all own up to our disobedience. The existence of boundary-breaking behavior does not mean we should shift the boundary lines. It doesn't change the truth that God has a plan for sexuality.

3

Not the Same

Why is sexual sin different from any other?

A Call to Humility

For the last several years, off and on, I (Ron) have walked with numerous men who have struggled with same-sex attraction and other sexual brokenness. I have had the joy of seeing God work in their lives, though I have not always been the best ambassador of God's love.

A few years ago, I was leading a small group of men who dealt with sexual sin of varying degrees, and each one wanted to be rid of the burden. Many were seeking purity and freedom from same-sex sin. It was a great group of broken men, and our glorious Savior and God was on the move. On one particular evening, as we were honestly confessing sin—the kind that keeps you up at night—a man in his early thirties spoke very frankly. His sexual sin was shocking, dark, and truly broken. Before I knew it, I blurted out: "You did what?"

I wish I hadn't said that.

He had been brutally honest, and I had been brutally insensitive. What I had forgotten in that moment was all the sexual sin that God had delivered me from. Yes, at the time I was living in purity, but it hadn't always been so. God had been at work in my life. He had done great things for me. I was free, thanks to him, but my freedom wasn't earned. It was sheer grace.

> For by grace you have been saved through faith. And this is not your own doing; it is the gift of God, not a result of works, so that no one may boast.
>
> Ephesians 2:8–9

Here Paul speaks to the church in Ephesus, and he makes it clear that their salvation is a gift. It is the result of God's action, through Christ, in their lives. It is not their doing. Salvation is *his* work.

So why do we start a chapter on why homosexual activity is sinful with a reminder of the sheer grace of God in Christ? Because we didn't write this chapter to give self-righteous men and women ammunition to throw at people. We write from the humble perspective that our lives have been touched by grace. We know that without Christ we would be living a life of misery or be dead. The same is true for you.

I hope Christ has done a good work in you. If so, praise God. As you read the rest of this chapter, remember that your life is the result of sheer grace. As we explore the particular ways homosexual activity is sinful, we do so in the hope that some will hear these words and cry out to Jesus—so that in their sin and brokenness, they too might know his sheer grace in their lives.[1]

I Remember

When I was a pagan, I lived as a pagan. I was deeply addicted to crystal meth and alcohol. My prohibitions were nearly nonexistent. I looked at pornography ceaselessly. I chatted with other men online. We would meet and have sex. Most times we would not even know each other's names. Sometimes, desperate, I would cruise and meet up with total strangers for sexual encounters. It was empty, dark, addictive, demonic, and so lonely. Flesh on flesh, but no intimacy. Two halves trying to be made whole. Never possible. Hungry but never satisfied. Aching but never finding relief. This was my life. Countless encounters, voyeuristic and exhibitionistic living, a harsh drug lifestyle. Surrounded by people but totally alone.

It was there in the hell of self, in my parents' garage, that Jesus encountered me in the summer of 1997. I was lonely, hungry, and afraid; the effects of my sin were taking their toll. He spoke so clearly to my heart that day—"Follow me or die." He wasn't harsh but he was clear. The life I was living would destroy me. There was no sugarcoating where I was at.

That day I said yes to Jesus. Looking back years later, I see the utter worthlessness of my pursuits. Having followed Jesus now for seventeen years, having known and walked with dozens of gay and lesbian friends seeking to follow Jesus, and being a lover of the Word of God, there is no doubt in my mind that homosexual acts are destructive, sinful, and far from God's best. Let me tell you why.

Two Alike Can Never Become One

The writer of Genesis declares, "Therefore a man shall leave his father and his mother and hold fast to his wife, and they shall become one flesh" (2:24). God's intent is for two very different human beings, a man and a woman, to come together and consummate their love in the sexual act. The two come together and become literally "one flesh." This beautiful intimacy of two "others" coming together mirrors, faintly, Christ's relationship with his bride, the church.[2] This complementarity is at the basis of sexual union and it is good. From it come pleasure, hope, and growth. Ben Patterson writes,

> God said of us that it is not good to be alone (Gen. 2:18). . . . Becoming "one flesh" is one of the truly unique features of a Christian understanding of marriage. Men and women are so very different from each other. . . . It is a lifelong adventure to love and understand this woman I live with—so very different from me and yet one with me. We have such a differing sexuality as male and female, we who are one and yet must become one! We have so much to learn from each other that it will take a lifetime! . . . Most of us have a lot to learn, and that is good—it draws us out of ourselves.[3]

This connection between a man and a woman is one of the most powerful goods that a human can experience in his or her life.

Paul is unwavering that those who engage in homosexual sin will be "consumed with passion" (Romans 1:27). His point is clear: At the base of homosexual activity is lust. It is the creature taking his or her needs in his or her own hands and seeking to fulfill them with someone that is just like himself. All it does is make a person hungry, make him or her want more. It is food that cannot satisfy. The more you eat, the hungrier you become.

In the brilliant book *The Lion, the Witch and the Wardrobe*, C. S. Lewis gets to this sober reality. Edmund, one of the children, is in Narnia and encounters the evil queen. He is cold and she offers him drink and food. He accepts. He asks for Turkish Delight. She gives it to him and he eats. And eats. Until it is all gone. Lewis writes,

> At last the Turkish Delight was all finished and Edmund was looking very hard at the empty box and wishing that she would ask him whether he would like some more. Probably the Queen

knew quite well what he was thinking; for she knew, though Edmund did not, that this was enchanted Turkish Delight and that anyone who had once tasted it would want more and more of it, and would even, if they were allowed, go on eating it till they killed themselves.[4]

In homosexual sexual activity, the participants may believe they are getting the good offered in Christian marriage; many believe that because they love one another, such a union will honor God. But instead of a relationship that sustains and forms the soul for holiness, what one gets is "Turkish Delight," a relationship that seems delightful but in the end will not achieve the purposes that God has ordained.

I experienced this firsthand in my own life. I had plenty of sexual experiences, plenty of unions, but none of it ever came close to the union that my wife and I have. Her otherness helps make me whole. It feeds me. It complements me. God is using it to bring about profound healing in my soul. He is so good. I am continually amazed that in the area of my life where I have experienced very deep conflict, darkness, and pain, I have experienced the great life of Jesus. Gay sexual encounters are two men or two women desperately seeking to become one in a way that is impossible. For them, the two can never become one.

Marriage for the Same-Sex Struggler

In the conversation about same-sex attraction, sin, and a Christian way forward, Christian marriage (between one man and one woman for life) is being seen as part of the problem. If you struggle, singleness is the only answer, some say. To get married in the midst of weakness now comes across as a plague to be avoided. Christian marriage used to be a viable option for those who need deep community and support in becoming holy.

Of course, singleness is a very valid choice for a Christian who struggles with same-sex attraction.[5] But so is marriage! One need not have porn-like lust for their spouse to have a beautiful, successful marriage. One can still have same-sex weakness and have a wonderful marriage.[6] A satisfying sex life is not the only measure of a good marriage. Martin Luther writes this about his wife: "I feel neither passionate love nor burning for my spouse, but I cherish her."[7] Now, I feel quite differently about my wife than he did about his, but the point is clear: Christian marriage is not fundamentally about sexual satisfaction. Martin Luther gets it right when he defines the purpose of marriage:

> The ultimate purpose is to obey God, to find aid and counsel against sin; to call upon God; to seek, love, and educate children for the glory of God; to live with one's wife in the fear of God and to bear the cross; but if there are no children, nevertheless to live with one's wife in contentment; and to avoid all lewdness with others.[8]

The Christian marriage that Luther speaks of so elegantly is available to the person struggling with same-sex desire. It will be quite an adventure, not lacking a few cliffs, but Christian marriage can be a place to "obey God" and find "contentment."

When we settle for same-sex unions as the best that God can do, we miss out on all the good that God wants to do. Scripture gives no allowance for same-sex union; it seems that only Christian marriage brings about the holiness, cross bearing, and contentment that Luther speaks of. To simply replace that with an untried alternative is a dangerous experiment.

Anti-Christ

The highest need of the human heart is to know Christ. No happiness, satisfaction, joy, or forgiveness is found apart from

Jesus. Many of us have heard well-meaning men and women who embrace their gay desire as their identity and say that they are gay Christians.[9] They declare that Christ embraces them as they embrace their gay identity as well as the sexual activity that comes from such identity. In fact, there is a huge push in some areas of the evangelical world to embrace such a theology.

Pastoral theologians such as Rob Bell and Brian McLaren trumpet a gospel that allows one to have both Jesus and one's prohibited lover. Both seem to think that Scripture allows for monogamous, committed homosexual relationships. For them, God is moving beyond the sexual ethics of the Bible to something totally new. These leaders are rewriting biblical sexuality and the morals that follow.

This ought to break our hearts. John Piper writes, "All sexual corruption serves to conceal the true knowledge of Christ."[10] Paul declares, "Or do you not know that the unrighteous will not inherit the kingdom of God? Do not be deceived: neither the sexually immoral, nor idolaters, nor adulterers, nor men who practice homosexuality . . . will inherit the kingdom of God" (1 Corinthians 6:9–10). Ongoing, unrepentant homosexual sin, along with a host of other sins, will keep people out of God's kingdom. It will keep them far from Christ. One of the primary reasons homosexual sin is devastating is because it keeps us from Jesus. It is a wide gulf that keeps us from being in relationship with him. To embrace such activity unrepentantly is to decide you do not want to be with Christ.

Other leaders in the church today are trying to integrate their personal struggle with same-sex attraction and their traditional understanding of sexuality. Some of these leaders try to bridge the gap between what the Bible teaches and what our current culture deems "acceptable" categories of experience. They hope to bring the identity language of *gay* and *lesbian* into the evangelical mainstream while advocating celibacy. Though preferable to embracing homosexual activity as holy, this mediating position is potentially problematic. There is not one biblical example of a person identifying with their sinful brokenness and then adding "Christian" to it. Could you imagine? I am an angry, unbelieving, porn-addicted Christian. Or, I am a lying Christian. This is what the Bible declares, "You are not your own, for you were bought with a price" (1 Corinthians 6:19–20). The only valid identification for a follower of Jesus is "disciple."[11]

In the midst of my sexual darkness, I chose again and again to walk away from Jesus and do what I wanted to do. I did not want his friendship, nor did I want the restraint of discipleship. I chose the identity that I wanted and I fully embraced it. Thankfully, I wasn't deceived into thinking I could have both. God spared me that deception. I knew that to engage in my sexual sin was to not be with Jesus. One cannot embrace his or her broken sexuality and at the same time seek to embrace Jesus. It is simply impossible. This is the sober reality of unrepentant homosexual activity: It is to starkly say no to Jesus.

Idolatry and Judgment

We (Ron and his family) live in the upper Midwest, and one of the things people do here in the fall is go apple-picking. So every year we take the kids and pick apples. We go to a huge apple orchard where there are thousands of trees and you can choose any kind of apple you like. Apples are the final product of a complex process. What happens inside the tree and at its root is what produces the fruit.

It is the same with our sexuality. The fruit of our sexuality (our behavior) is the final product of a complex process that happens inside our hearts and minds. It is what is inside us—at our root—that is the problem. And at the root of homosexuality is idolatry.[12] If left untreated, it will produce bad fruit. It is this root and fruit that will bring God's judgment. Consider Paul's words:

> Claiming to be wise, they became fools, and exchanged the glory of the immortal God for images resembling mortal man and birds and animals and creeping things. Therefore God gave them up in the lusts of their hearts to impurity, to the dishonoring of their bodies among themselves, because they exchanged the truth about God for a lie and worshiped and served the creature rather than the Creator, who is blessed forever! Amen. For this reason God gave them up to dishonorable passions.
>
> Romans 1:22–26

In addition, Paul says, "For the wrath of God is revealed from heaven against all ungodliness and unrighteousness of men, who by their unrighteousness suppress the truth" (Romans 1:18). At the root of homosexuality is idolatry—worshiping the creature over the Creator. It is to throw out God's order and design and to engage in behavior that demeans his creation. Such living will bring his wrath.

But all this is of little consequence compared to the eternal ramifications of unrepentant sexual idolatry. A day will come when every person, gay and straight, will stand before the Creator and give an account of their sin, sexual or otherwise. And to those who have lived unrepentant lives, there will be judgment that will last forever. But thank God that there is hope. God in Christ can bring about the total redemption of a gay or lesbian person.

All they must do is desire it and ask him to do it.

Conclusion

We need to talk about the sinfulness of homosexuality with humility. We all are sinful and capable of horrendous sin. It is by the grace of God that any are saved. But make no mistake, homosexual activity is a sin: In homosexual activity, there is no union as described in Scripture; there are not the benefits found in monogamous, heterosexual relationships; any attempt to claim to be Christian and to continue in homosexual practice is contrary to the gospel. Finally, homosexual idolatry, like other sins, will bring judgment. Thankfully, God, in and through Christ, has made a way for redemption for any person who wants it and asks for it.

Many pastors and theologians are arguing that if the act of homosexuality really is sinful, it is about as bad as gluttony. It might not make us many friends, but someone needs to speak the tough truth: Homosexuality is different. Eating too much pie is not the same as same-sex sexual activity. Who we are as sexual beings and what we do with our bodies affects us in unique, eternal ways.

4

Jesus Is My Homeboy

If he didn't care, why should we?

If you really want to discover the religion that drives our culture, visit your local mall. If marketers with master's degrees are paid millions of dollars to study us and figure out how to sell *these* things in *this* way, what does that tell us? One walk-through will reveal more than you probably want to know about what we value, the things that tempt us, and the gods we worship.

On a trip like this I (Adam) realized that our post-Christian culture, far from rejecting Jesus, fancies him enough to put him on T-shirts. Shuffling past one of those edgy, goth/skater/"rebel with a credit limit" shops, I was shocked to see a "Jesus is my homeboy" shirt on the wall. Like a screen print icon, the Son of God was depicted flashing a big grin with two thumbs up and some pretty dope bling. In that moment, I realized that almost everyone thinks Jesus is all right—not just the Doobie Brothers.

I also realized something about the power of sin in our hearts. The fact is, when we're driven by selfishness, we desperately want a Jesus who will take our side, defend our opinions, and make us comfortable with ourselves. We love Jesus, as long as he conforms to our image!

Today, revisionist interpreters are trying to convince us that Jesus is neutral toward homosexuality. In essential ways, they are repainting the Christian faith. We need to be careful. *Very careful!* If there is anything more dangerous than simply rejecting Jesus as Lord, it is bowing down to an idol of our making and calling it *Jesus*.

Using Jesus

Out of 31,102 Bible verses, only seven frequently quoted verses (none the words of Jesus) speak directly of same-sex behavior—and mostly in the context of idolatry, temple prostitution, adultery, child exploitation, or violence.[1]

—David Myers, Professor of Psychology

Presidential candidate Barack Obama has written in *The Audacity of Hope* . . . that he is not "willing to accept a reading of the Bible that considers an obscure line in Romans [about homosexual practice] to be more defining of Christianity than the Sermon on the Mount." He repeated this line in a campaign appearance in Ohio this past March. He stated that if people find controversial his views on granting the full benefits of marriage to homosexual unions, minus only the name, "then I would just refer them to the Sermon on the Mount, which I think is, in my mind, for my faith, more central than an obscure passage in Romans."[2]

As a kid, one of the best plans I ever hatched to get my way involved creative questions and loose interpretations. It worked something like this: I went to my mom and asked, "Mom, if Dad says I'm allowed to ride my bike into town and get some candy, is that okay with you too?" Mom, trusting Dad to hold the line, replied, "Sure." Then, I asked Dad the same question. Dad, trusting Mom to make the call, said, "Sure." With a bit of subtle harmonizing, I determined I had received permission. It was a variation on the old "pit Mom and Dad against each other" tactic. Looking back, I feel guilty.

When we first encounter the argument "You know, Jesus never talked about homosexuality," it is easy to be intimidated. After all, he (technically) never did. When we add to that little revelation the assertion that "only seven frequently quoted Bible verses" ever condemn homosexuality, it is even easier to wonder, "Wow . . . maybe Jesus doesn't care about this issue."

But this is just another version of the old "pit Mom against Dad" tactic. In this case, someone is trying to pit Jesus against the rest of the Bible, or pit the rest of the Bible against seven passages (more on this in chapter 5). As we will see, if careful interpretation is our goal, the tactic doesn't really work.

Frankly, it is sort of troubling to see people use Jesus as a mascot for their "team." We suppose it is understandable, but it certainly is not laudable. Jesus never offers to be our hobbyhorse or serve our ideology.

Jesus deserves our worship, adoration, and humble submission. Rather than using Jesus to prove a point, in this chapter, we want to take some time to truly understand him. First, we want to clear up the idea that Jesus was neutral toward or even affirming of same-sex relationships. Second, we want to see how Jesus showed us what it really looks like to be open and affirming.

Jesus, the Bible, and Homosexuality

The revisionist argument is simple and straightforward: Because Jesus never spoke about homosexuality, and because he emphasized love and acceptance, his example trumps other biblical passages about homosexuality. Since Christians look to Jesus as our ultimate example, we should be open-minded and accepting. We can offer three reasons that this understanding of Jesus is wrong.

1. This argument tries to drive a wedge between Jesus and the Bible he inspired.

In several places, Scripture clearly condemns same-sex relations. Here are four (read carefully):

You shall not lie with a male as with a woman; it is an abomination.

Leviticus 18:22

If a man lies with a male as with a woman, both of them have committed an abomination; they shall surely be put to death; their blood is upon them.

Leviticus 20:13

For this reason, God gave them up to dishonorable passions. For their women exchanged natural relations for those that are contrary to nature; and the men likewise gave up natural relations with women and were consumed with passion for one another, men committing shameless acts with men and receiving in themselves the due penalty for their error.

Romans 1:26–27

Do you not know that the unrighteous will not inherit the kingdom of God? Do not be deceived: neither the sexually immoral, nor idolaters, nor adulterers, nor men who practice homosexuality, nor thieves, nor the greedy, nor drunkards, nor revilers, nor swindlers will inherit the kingdom of God. And such were some of you. But you were washed, you were sanctified, you were justified in the name of the Lord Jesus Christ and by the Spirit of our God.

1 Corinthians 6:9–11

We will look at these verses more closely in chapter 5. For now, we note the obvious: Scripture does not affirm homosexual acts. It speaks out strongly, calling them unrighteous and an abomination. Within the Old Testament community, homosexual activity was grounds for the death penalty.[3] This is serious language. How do revisionist interpreters go about reinterpreting these passages?

They begin by arguing that Jesus' example trumps the passages traditionalists use to condemn homosexuality. According to the revisionists, if we want to get to the essence of Christianity, we should look to Jesus. If he was open and affirming, then the "clobber passages" no longer apply.[4] This revisionist argument works by trying to drive a wedge between Jesus and the rest of the Bible, but Jesus does not treat the Bible that way.

In John 10, Jesus declares that "Scripture cannot be broken" (v. 35). This is Jesus' way of saying that Scripture is *always* true. In other words, the Bible doesn't have an expiration date. When quoting the Old Testament, Jesus frequently says "God says . . ."—equating the words of the Old Testament with God's words. For Jesus, when Scripture speaks, God is speaking.

This intimate connection is further clarified as we consider something else: The Bible teaches that Jesus himself inspired Scripture, making sure the entire Old Testament would point toward him and the entire New Testament would bear witness to his coming. For example, in 1 Peter 1:11, the apostle tells us that "the Spirit of Christ" moved Old Testament authors to write about Jesus. That is a stunning claim: Long before he takes on human flesh, Jesus speaks through the biblical authors, leading them to describe what he would be like, what he would teach, and what he would do to reconcile humanity to God![5]

While "red letter" Bibles make it easier to identify the words Jesus preached on the shores of Galilee, they can obscure an important reality: Jesus inspired every word of Scripture! In an ultimate sense, *every* letter of our Bibles could be red.

There is no two-tiered Bible or canon within a canon. Scripture reveals God's thoughts with consistency and coherence. In the end, the revisionist interpretation gets Jesus wrong because it tries to do the impossible. We *can't* drive a wedge between Jesus and the Bible because Jesus inspired and fulfilled its message.

2. The revisionist assertion is an "argument from silence," a dodgy tactic in philosophical discussions.

The revisionist argument is simple: Because Jesus didn't directly address homosexuality he must not have been opposed to it. This is a perfect example of an "argument from silence." This common philosophical error falters by assuming a person's silence on an issue indicates they are indifferent to it. That's some seriously flawed logic.

It reminds us of "The Great Platonic Greek Debate." Maybe you haven't heard of it. Here's the scoop: Did you realize that there is not one single sentence in all of Plato's writings that tells us he spoke Greek? Scholars are hotly debating the implications of this silence on Plato's language preference. Perhaps he spoke Aramaic. Or maybe he dialogued in some unknown barbarian tongue. Unless they are able to find some place in his writings that affirms he spoke Greek, the question will remain unanswered.

Of course . . . there is no such thing as "The Great Platonic Greek Debate." In fact, no one doubts that Plato spoke Greek.

Though history is silent on the subject, we're absolutely confident he spoke it. We know Plato was Greek. We have copies of his work, entirely penned in Greek. Simply put, silence on the topic does not call his Greek-speaking preference into question!

In a similar way, Jesus' silence on the specific issue of homosexuality is really not informative at all. It certainly should not lead us to think that a first-century rabbi, like Jesus, would have rejected the sexual ethic of the Old Testament. Because Jesus believed the Old Testament was God's Word and because Jesus, like the entire Jewish community of his day, looked to the moral code of the Old Testament, and because we know, theologically speaking, that Jesus inspired its authorship, we can be sure Jesus would not endorse homosexuality.

But we have more than that.

3. When diagnosing sexual sin, Jesus always pointed people back to God's design plan.

It is interesting to see how Jesus dealt with other aspects of sexual ethics. For instance, when he was asked about divorce (Matthew 19:1–12), Jesus could easily have pointed to some texts that specifically condemn wrongful divorce.[6] For example, Malachi 2:16, "The man who . . . divorces [his wife] . . . covers his garment with violence, says the Lord of hosts. So guard yourselves in your spirit, and do not be faithless." This ringing condemnation of wrongful divorce could have been helpful.

But Jesus did not turn there. Instead, he pointed people back to Genesis 2 and the one-flesh union (see chapter 1). In other words, Jesus made a critical point: If you want to know what sin is, check out the design plan—one man, one woman, a lifetime covenant. For Jesus, anything outside this arrangement would be one item on a long list that could be summarized by the phrase *sexual immorality*. While Jesus never specifically pointed out homosexuality, any time he referenced "sexual immorality," homosexuality would certainly have been one expression of the sin he had in mind. In the words of New Testament scholar Robert Gagnon:

> The idea that Jesus was, or might have been, personally neutral or even affirming of homosexual conduct is revisionist history at its worst. . . . The portrayal of Jesus as a first-century Palestinian Jew who was open to homosexual practice is simply ahistorical. All the evidence leads in the opposite direction. . . . He also did not address other sexual issues such as incest and bestiality, but that hardly indicates a neutral or positive stance on such matters. . . . Jesus, both in what he says and what he fails to say, remains squarely on the side of those who reject homosexual practice.[7]

What We Can Learn From Jesus' Example

Jesus is more than a trump card to be played against those who promote a revisionist understanding of Scripture. The Lord shows us what it looks like to reach out to all people. Jesus exercised radical love that confronts our hardhearted judgmentalism. He spoke life-transforming truth, calling us to submit our lives to God's rule. Here are two specific ways Jesus shows us how to reach out to the homosexual community.

1. Jesus was a radically inclusive barrier breaker.

Jesus did a lot of things to irritate the religious establishment of his day. They were probably offended when he called them sons of the devil (John 8). It is safe to say that their apple cart was overturned when he cleansed the temple, single-handedly driving out a gaggle of money-changers and animal vendors . . . twice (John 2; Matthew 21).

One of the things that most offended them was Jesus' complete disregard for their carefully segregated social order. When it came to exploding barriers based on gender, race, and religion, Jesus was walking TNT. Consider three of his famous encounters.

A Roman soldier

In Matthew 8, while visiting Capernaum, Jesus is approached by a centurion whose servant is sick at home. When Jesus offers to come to the man's house and heal the servant, the centurion replies,

> Lord, I am not worthy to have you come under my roof, but only say the word, and my servant will be healed. For I too am a man under authority, with soldiers under me. And I say to one, "Go," and he goes, and to another, "Come," and he comes, and to my servant, "Do this," and he does it.
>
> vv. 8–9

Jesus, marveling at the faith of the centurion, heals the servant.

Consider something that might be easy to miss: The soldier was willing to approach Jesus. Any Roman on assignment in Judea would have known that Jews viewed his people with hostility. The Romans were an unwelcome occupying army. Yet this man saw something in Jesus, a hospitality that bridged obvious barriers. The story concludes as Jesus delivers a shocking pronouncement:

> I tell you, many will come from east and west and recline at table with Abraham, Isaac, and Jacob in the kingdom of heaven, while the sons of the kingdom will be thrown into the outer darkness. In that place there will be weeping and gnashing of teeth.
>
> vv. 11–12

A MIRACULOUS MEAL

In Mark 8, we find Jesus teaching the gospel to a vast crowd, more than four thousand people. He is in a Gentile area, so the crowd was probably mixed, Jews and Gentiles together. Looking out over the crowd, Jesus realizes they need food, so taking a few loaves and fish, he miraculously feeds the multitude.

Setting aside the Wow!-factor miracle of multiplying the loaves and fishes, what does this story tell us about Jesus' heart? First, that his compassion was not reserved only for the "right kind" of people. In his kingdom, Jesus wanted to see the needs of Jew and Gentile equally met. There is more.

Mealtimes were unique in Jewish culture. In fact, the phrase *break bread* carried a significance among Jews that was not shared in the same way by the Greco-Roman culture of the day. Mealtime was a *family* occasion. The father would stand, bless the food, and break a loaf of bread. There was something sacramental about the whole thing, pointing to God's provision in their lives.[8]

This was not a time to mix with non-Jews. Not only would outsiders not "get it" when it came to their customs and understanding of the meal, Jews worried about becoming ritually unclean. Their anxiety could be compared to our fear of sitting across the table from someone with the flu. We don't want to get what they've got!

At the feeding of the four thousand, Jesus stands, blesses the food, breaks the bread, and passes it out. In this simple action, he is inviting Gentiles to join with Jews in a family meal. Jesus is allowing them to receive the blessings that, according to the experts, were reserved for Abraham's children alone.[9]

This bugged the religious establishment.

A SINNER'S PARTY

In Mark 2, we read about Jesus calling Matthew (also known as Levi) to be one of his disciples. Interestingly, Matthew is serving as a tax collector, one of the more despised occupations in history. Among his fellow Jews, Matthew would have been viewed as a shill for the Roman authority, a representative of "The Man." Yet Jesus chooses him, inviting Matthew to discover a new master.

Then Jesus goes a step further.

Matthew invites him over to a party with his friends. You know the saying, "Birds of a feather . . ." Well, Matthew liked to hang out with other tax collectors and sinners. Before meeting Jesus, he was one of them! A whole subset of unrighteousness is covered under the term *sinner*—the word Mark uses to describe Matthew's friends—prostitution, promiscuity, drunkenness, theft, and so on. In the Jewish context at this time, associating with one of these people could transfer ritual impurity to a righteous person.

For example, there was a group of radically devoted people called the Essenes. They believed that when the Messiah arrived he would destroy all the unrighteous Gentiles, chastise the less righteous Jews, and elevate the Essenes, who had kept the rules. We actually have writings from these people. In one scroll, there is a serious debate about whether a ritually clean water pitcher could be made unclean if used to pour water into an unclean water cup. They seriously worried that the "uncleanness" would travel up the water stream and into the pitcher.

It sounds crazy, but these concerns filled the minds of religious leaders who watched Jesus break bread with sinners. In that simple act of sharing a meal, the Lord was giving us an example of what it means to be inclusive. It means drawing the circle of our compassion widely, not narrowly. It means sharing life with people who might not yet know the Way, the Truth, and the Life.

2. In his call to discipleship, Jesus demanded unqualified repentance and true faith.

At the same time, it was clear that Jesus' liberal, wide-armed embrace of anyone who truly sought him was not to be mistaken with a wide-open gate into the kingdom. His welcoming hospitality was never meant to be confused with an indifference to the lifestyle of those who asked to follow him. If they wanted life in his kingdom, it meant true repentance—death to the former self—and genuine faith in Jesus as Lord.[10]

The same Jesus who ate with sinners, healed their diseases, and willingly faced down the condemnation of the religious establishment, also made something clear: God is going to judge sin. The good news Jesus brought was *not* that the bar was going to be set lower than the Pharisees described. In fact, the bar was much higher than they had imagined! In the same way that Jesus widened the circle of God's compassionate love and mercy, he also widened our understanding of God's demands.

MARK 8:34-38: DISCIPLESHIP DEFINED

And calling the crowd to him with his disciples, he said to them, "If anyone would come after me, let him deny himself and take up his cross and follow me. For whoever would save his life will lose it, but whoever loses his life for my sake and the gospel's will save it. For what does it profit a man to gain the whole world and forfeit his soul? For what can a man give in return for his soul? For whoever is ashamed of me and of my words in this adulterous and sinful generation, of him will the Son of Man also be ashamed when he comes in the glory of his Father with the holy angels."

We should notice how Mark distinguishes the two groups—"the crowd" and "his disciples." During Jesus' earthly ministry, there were many people in the crowd. Jesus fed them. He taught them. He may even have healed some of them. But membership in the crowd didn't make them disciples. Jesus clearly taught them and us what it means to move from being in the crowd to becoming a disciple.

At the heart of discipleship is a self-denying submission to Jesus as Lord. Jesus describes a disciple as someone who has "taken up his cross." In the Roman world, only condemned criminals carried crosses. People carrying crosses were not thinking about laundry or shopping. They were not concerned with a job promotion or the next step in self-actualization. They were on *one* path—to the place of execution.

The road to *true* life will sometimes feel like death. Disciples must be willing to say no to desires that seem undeniable and irresistible. We must say no to deep longings that seem to define who we are. In other words, someone who wants to follow Jesus can't be committed to charting their own course in life. They surrender/crucify that right. They proclaim, "My way of doing things doesn't work. I deny my right to self-define and self-direct."

Many people are more than happy to follow the peaceful Jesus, the generous Jesus, and the compassionate Jesus. But when Jesus says, "Follow me," he is calling us to acknowledge his authority, his kingship. If we want to be part of his kingdom, we must make him our King. Every person who steps out of the crowd to follow Jesus must tread this cruciform path, denying self in obedience to the Savior. When our will and his are in conflict, he demands our submission.

And that brings us back to the relationship between Jesus and the rest of the Bible. Scripture is really the revelation of our King's will. It is the perfect, inspired decree of the man from Nazareth who ate with sinners, healed centurions' servants, and told us that *anyone* was welcome to come follow him. There is only one condition: *He* gets to be King.[11] We cannot call Jesus Lord if we ignore his Word.

The good news of Scripture is that we can reach out with an arms-wide-open love to our gay friends and neighbors. We are not called to a "ministry of shunning." On the contrary, we should find appropriate ways to open our lives and build relationships. At the same time, we need to be clear about what true discipleship entails—walking the King's way. And that way is one that will sometimes feel like death. If we are walking that path ourselves, then we can speak with the humility of those who are struggling to put to death the sin in our own lives.

5

Ban All Shrimp

Shouldn't conservatives be consistent in their reading of Scripture?

In our last chapter, we focused on demonstrating that Jesus would never have dismissed the Bible's teaching on homosexuality. In essence, we argued that we can't drive a wedge between Jesus and Scripture. To make that point, we assumed you would grant us, for the sake of argument, that the rest of the Bible clearly prohibits sexual relations that violate God's blueprint for intimacy: one man, one woman, a lifetime covenant of marriage. In this chapter, we want to make it clear that the Bible consistently presents this message in both the Old and New Testaments.

Revisionist interpreters have a difficult—we would say impossible—task: Somehow, they must take the most clear condemnations of homosexual activity and convince us that these don't condemn homosexual activity.

The "Wrong" Part of the Bible?

You shall not lie with a male as with a woman; it is an abomination.

Leviticus 18:22

If a man lies with a male as with a woman, both of them have committed an abomination; they shall surely be put to death; their blood is upon them.

Leviticus 20:13

Living in Tension

The church has always faced a tension when it comes to the Old Testament: We believe it is part of the Bible, but we wonder how it continues to apply to us. After all, Jesus brought us salvation by grace, through faith alone. Gentiles don't have to walk through the doorway of Judaism to become disciples of Jesus (see Acts 15). On the other hand, the God who revealed himself in Jesus Christ inspired the Old Testament.

This tension is relevant to discussion of these two key passages in Leviticus. Each speaks clear condemnation of same-sex behavior. The most basic way revisionist interpreters write off these passages is by pointing out, "They're in Leviticus, a part of the Bible that doesn't apply anymore." For example, Lisa Miller comments:

> The Bible does condemn gay male sex in a handful of passages. Twice Leviticus refers to sex between men as "an abomination" . . . but these are throwaway lines in a peculiar text given over to codes for living in the ancient Jewish world, a text that devotes verse after verse to treatments for leprosy, cleanliness rituals for menstruating women, and the correct way to sacrifice a goat. . . . Most of us no longer heed Leviticus on haircuts or blood sacrifices; our modern understanding of the world has surpassed its prescriptions.[1]

Her point is simple: Because these passages are part of the Holiness Code, they are irrelevant to the discussion. The argument goes like this: Clearly we live as if parts of the Old Testament no longer matter. We mix our linens and wools. We eat bacon (thank God!). We don't wear tassels on our coats. The question is poignant: Are the shrimp-eating[2] Christians who use passages in Leviticus to condemn homosexual practice acting like total hypocrites? We need to pick: Either we follow it all, or we ignore it all.

As fathers in our own families, Ron and I (Adam) have learned something: Our children often want things nice, neat, and simple. They can be quick to jump on *any* perceived point of ambiguity. Like seasoned lawyers, they can call out with passion unfairness and inconsistency. Sometimes, parents simply answer, "It's that way because I said so." Sometimes, we give a more detailed explanation. It doesn't take long to realize that if our kids don't like what we're saying, they will do *anything* they can to utilize an apparent contradiction.

Mature people, on the other hand, are more concerned with discovering truth than exploiting a perceived inconsistency. They realize that a person with intellectual integrity, speaking about a variety of things over a long period of time, will inevitably state two things that might *appear* contradictory. When we come across such a situation, honest interpreters will lay aside ideological axes, cease spinning their grinding wheels, and put on their thinking caps. Christians will be driven by a deep confidence that our truth-speaking God would never contradict himself!

When interpreting Scripture, it is a mistake to claim that every passage in the Holiness Code is equally timeless and applicable. It is also a mistake to claim any passage that happens to be located in the Holiness Code is automatically irrelevant! God won't allow his Word to be pressed into these easy either-or categories. Instead, it will take a careful, honest study of the relevant texts to understand how they fit together.

Reading More Carefully

So what should we do with these two passages in Leviticus? Let's begin by observing a few things about the *content* of these verses. They specifically deal with two men engaging in sexual acts. The text does not refer to a man and a youth, or a man with his servant. The author had three Hebrew words at his disposal, and he chose the one that refers most broadly to men. In other words, he is talking about consenting adults.

Second, we should note something about the *context* of these verses. Revisionists often point to some of the commandments in the Holiness Code that no longer apply (like dietary restrictions or clothing regulations). At the same time, in the immediate context of these two verses, things like incest, bestiality, and child sacrifice are specifically condemned. Of the many sexual sins listed here (Leviticus 18:6–30; 20:10–21)—activities we would *still* consider sinful[3]—sexual intimacy between two men is specifically condemned as an "abomination" (18:22) and, along with other perversions, subject to the death penalty (20:13).[4] Is it possible to distinguish between strands of this code that have been discontinued now that we are in Christ, and parts of it that still provide moral guidance for today?

That is exactly what Paul does in the New Testament. It is worth noting that of all the New Testament authors, Paul most strenuously argued for a better understanding of the Law. His entire letter to the Galatians is a warning that those who seek to be made right with God by obeying the Law will be condemned.[5] At the same time, he also insisted that the Law was a gospel-essential, God-given revelation.[6] Paul provides a perfect example of what it looks like to remain rooted in truth without ranging into extremes.

Just as Paul rejects the extreme position of assuming every prescription in the Holiness Code is eternally relevant (his entire letter to the Galatian church is a case in point), his example warns against the opposite extreme, assuming that everything in the Holiness Code is irrelevant. While clearly teaching that the Law cannot justify, Paul *explicitly drew* from the Levitical Law when teaching about sexual purity. For example:

- In 1 Corinthians 5, Paul argues against incest, echoing the incest laws of Leviticus 18 and, in some cases, using language that is basically the same.
- In Romans 1:32, Paul describes homosexual practice, and other sins, as "worthy of death" (KJV), echoing the death penalty of Leviticus 20:13.
- In Romans 1:27, Paul uses a Greek word *aschemosyne* ("indecency, indecent exposure"), which is used twenty-four times in the Greek version of Leviticus 18:6–19 to describe sinful sexual acts.
- Paul also uses the same word as Leviticus 18:19 for "impurity" in Romans 1:24.

Perhaps the most important place we see Paul draw from the Holiness Code in addressing sexual behavior comes in 1 Corinthians 6:9–10:

> Or do you not know that the unrighteous will not inherit the kingdom of God? Do not be deceived: neither the sexually immoral, nor idolaters, nor adulterers, nor men who practice homosexuality, nor thieves, nor the greedy, nor drunkards, nor revilers, nor swindlers will inherit the kingdom of God.

In Greek, the phrase *men who practice homosexuality* is actually one word: *arsenokoites*. Strictly translated, it means "men who lie with men." It is a word that Paul himself formed by putting together two Greek words, *arsen* and *koites*. Interestingly, these two words stand side by side in the Greek translation of Leviticus 20:13.[7] In other words, Paul, writing under the inspiration of the Holy Spirit, explicitly endorses the condemnation of homosexual sex in Leviticus.[8]

We would draw three implications:

1. Though parts of the Holiness Code are no longer applicable, we should tread softly when God speaks of certain practices in very strong terms.

2. While the immediate context of the Leviticus passage is important, it is equally important to take the entire Bible as relevant to discussion. Because Paul drew specifically on this passage, its moral teaching still applies today.

3. Though Paul does not call for the death penalty to be applied to practicing homosexuals, he retains the condemning language that such behavior is "worthy of death." In other words, while Paul is not prescribing a law code for civil authorities to impose penalties, he unflinchingly articulates the severity of God's judgment.[9]

Essentially, the revisionist argues that the *canonical context* of the Leviticus passages makes them irrelevant. Because they appear in a certain part of the Old Testament, they are no longer binding. We have seen that the story is not so simple. A more careful, nuanced reading of the text shows us that, in fact, Paul specifically drew from these sections of the Old Testament when framing his own teaching on homosexual acts.

The "Wrong" Understanding of Homosexuality?

For this reason God gave them up to dishonorable passions. For their women exchanged natural relations for those that are contrary to nature; and the men likewise gave up natural relations with women and were consumed with passion for one another, men committing shameless acts with men and receiving in themselves the due penalty for their error.

Romans 1:26–27

If the revisionist argument against the Leviticus passages is about *canon*, their argument against Romans is about *culture*. To those who would quote Leviticus, they would reply, "Irrelevant part of the Old Testament." To those who would quote Romans 1, they would say, "Irrelevant, culturally uninformed understanding of homosexuality." How does this argument work?

It begins by suggesting that Paul is not talking about a loving, mutual relationship between two homosexual adults. Instead, the argument runs, he is condemning the ancient practice of pederasty (older men sleeping with boys), a common practice in the ancient world. According to the revisionist, Paul speaks out against these exploitative sex acts, not "normal" homosexual intimacy.

Further, they argue, Paul is specifically calling out people for being consumed with lust. They are being condemned for their idolatry of sex. They are driven by "dishonorable passions" to commit "shameless acts." The issue, the revisionist claims, is not the gender of the sexual partners, but the way they go about their sex lives.

Finally, the typical revisionist argument suggests that Paul simply does not understand human sexuality. Paul did not really have the proper categories to talk about homosexual relationships. Specifically, he did not understand the science of "sexual orientation." Writing long before 1973, when the American Psychological Association responded to pressure from protesters and removed same-sex attraction from its manual of psychological disorders, Paul did not have an informed reference point for homosexual experience. In our day, the argument runs, we understand that some people are simply oriented toward members of the same sex. Their desire for intimacy with members of the same sex is not inordinate lust, but natural affection.

There are a number of problems with these arguments. The most significant is that the majority of those who strongly argue in favor of normalizing homosexual behavior do not pretend that Paul can be used in support of their perspective. In other words, they acknowledge that they are at loggerheads with Paul's clear condemnation of homosexuality.

For example, in *Homoeroticism in the Biblical World,* Martti Nissinen writes,

> Paul does not mention . . . female and male persons who were habitually involved in homoerotic relationships; but if he knew about them (and there is every reason to believe he did), it is difficult to think that, because of their apparent "orientation," he would *not* have included them in Romans 1:26–27. . . . For him, there is no individual inversion or inclination that would make this conduct less culpable. . . . Presumably nothing would have made Paul approve homoerotic behavior.[10]

Louis Crompton, in *Homosexuality and Civilization*, provides a massive treatment of homosexuality in the ancient world. He comments,

> According to [one] interpretation, Paul's words were not directed at "bona fide" homosexuals in committed relationships. But such a reading, however well-intentioned, seems strained and unhistorical. Nowhere does Paul or any other Jewish writer of this period imply the least acceptance of same-sex relations under any circumstance. The idea that homosexuals might be redeemed by mutual devotion would have been wholly foreign to Paul or any other Jew or early Christian.[11]

Each of these authors supports full inclusion for same-sex intimacy. At the same time, they are careful scholars, experts in their field who clearly understand that Paul meant what he said in Romans 1.

Conclusion: One Message

If we really want to love someone, we need to value them for who they are. In any human relationship, someone who demonstrates little interest in truly understanding his friend probably isn't a true friend. When we take time to hear someone, value what they communicate, and interpret what they say with a commitment to letting them speak on their own terms, we are honoring them. The same applies to Scripture. If we come to the Bible bound and determined to have things our way, then we will likely find some way to make it say what we want it to say.

It is moving to realize just how many revisionist interpreters have a personal stake in this issue. Many of them have children who have struggled with same-sex desire or good friends and colleagues in the LGBT community. Some explicitly affirm that their reinterpretation of Scripture was motivated by the realization that a loved one is gay.

We should all sympathize with the anguish such circumstances ushered into the lives of these authors and teachers. According to those who have shared their stories, they felt they faced a choice between loving and accepting their friend/child/peer, or communicating some level of rejection by embracing the historical biblical interpretation. It is difficult to imagine their sense of inner conflict.

Yet, in some ways, we can do more than imagine. For Ron, the struggle was not simply whether or not he could accept a loved one, but what it meant to be himself. For both of us, good people dealing with deep issues come into our lives on a regular basis in pastoral ministry.

The reality is every single person who comes to the Bible has some kind of agenda. We are all writing a story with our lives, so when we come to the text of Scripture, we want to understand, "What kind of story will my life become if I allow this book to guide me?" When Scripture's message confronts and challenges us, when it speaks an uncomfortable truth, part of us is facing a hard choice: Am I willing to let the Bible rewrite my story, or will I attempt to rewrite the Bible?

We realize that this is a simplistic way of describing the choices that face every biblical interpreter. We are not trying to pen a scholarly treatise on hermeneutics (i.e., interpretation theory). At the same time, we think this question of commitment lies at the headwaters of all interpretive endeavor, whether we are using our PhD to craft a revised interpretation of biblical doctrine, or rifling through Scripture to find passages to affirm a gay son or daughter, or abusing the Bible to justify our prejudice, or cherry-picking passages to support our political agenda, or naming and claiming certain out-of-context passages to get that brand-new BMW, or . . . you get the point.

Each of us must determine whether we are willing to give this Book its way. Will Scripture have the right to edit us? In the end, everyone who calls Jesus Lord must be willing to submit the story of their lives to the story of God's Book. We must come from our world into this Word with a deep trust that it may call us into difficulty, trial, even death to self. But our ultimate hope is to let it so mark our lives that one consistent message might be proclaimed through us: the gospel.

Takeaway

We examined a key claim made by revisionist Bible interpreters: The passages that seem to speak the most clearly against homosexuality no longer apply. Increasingly people claim that conservatives practice selective interpretation to bolster their biases, but we saw that Scripture speaks with a uniform voice when it comes to homosexual activity. It is not God's plan.

6

Perception and Reality

How can homosexuals trust Christians when they act like a bunch of homophobes?

Five years ago I (Ron) was getting ready to preach. An hour before the service, one of our young adults came to me and asked for a hurried meeting. With determination, he told me he was gay and that he was coming out. He had decided to be a gay Christian. No more struggle, no more questions, he had found who he truly was. I had no idea that he had been dealing with this issue. He had been part of our community and didn't feel safe enough or bold enough to share the reality of what was going on within his soul. I told him my story. I sought to keep the conversation going, but he was done. His heart was hardened, and he soon changed churches.

I have had numerous friendships with men and women who are dealing with homosexuality. Many of the relationships have gone better than the story above. But I have also made many mistakes—reacting with anger and fear. For me, there has been a steep learning curve. I think this is true for the church as well.

David Kinnaman, in his book *unChristian*, shows us the landscape we find ourselves in:

> Out of twenty attributes that we assessed, both positive and negative, as they related to Christianity, the perception of being anti-homosexual was at the top of the list. More than nine out of ten Mosaic and Buster outsiders (91 percent) said "anti-homosexual" accurately describes present-day Christianity. And two-thirds of outsiders have very strong opinions about Christians in this regard, easily generating the largest group of vocal critics.[1]

He goes on to say, "When most of us engage homosexuals, we come across as arrogant, self-righteous, and uncaring—the opposite of how Jesus engaged outsiders."[2] Whether right or wrong, the church has work to do.

Like many evangelicals, I have strong feelings about homosexuality. There is no doubt in my mind that homosexual activity, in any form, is sin. Homosexuality isn't just a secondary issue like what version of the Bible we should read. Instead, it touches upon core issues of the Christian faith and doctrine. But I am afraid that in our right pursuit of orthodoxy, we have found, perhaps unwittingly, a way of saying that "those people" just aren't welcome here.

Almost all of us, in the days ahead, will interact with gays and lesbians either in the church or in our daily lives. With so much in the culture an anathema to the gospel, it would be easy to get defensive, scared, and reactive. Thankfully, the Bible teaches us a way of living that is faithful and kind.

A Good Story

In Luke, chapter 10, Jesus encounters a lawyer.

> And behold, a lawyer stood up to put him to the test, saying, "Teacher, what shall I do to inherit eternal life?" He said to

him, "What is written in the Law? How do you read it?" And he answered, "You shall love the Lord your God with all your heart and with all your soul and with all your strength and with all your mind, and your neighbor as yourself." And he said to him, "You have answered correctly; do this, and you will live."

But he, desiring to justify himself, said to Jesus, "And who is my neighbor?"

Luke 10:25–29

Many people mistake this moment in the gospel as a teaching about how to obtain eternal life, but the story of the Good Samaritan is not about salvation. Instead, Jesus uses a parable to answer the question *"Who is my neighbor?"* In this great narrative, we learn who our neighbor is and how we should love him.

This is the story Jesus tells the lawyer about who his neighbor is:

Jesus replied, "A man was going down from Jerusalem to Jericho, and he fell among robbers, who stripped him and beat him and departed, leaving him half dead. Now by chance a priest was going down that road, and when he saw him he passed by on the other side. So likewise a Levite, when he came to the place and saw him, passed by on the other side. But a Samaritan, as he journeyed, came to where he was, and when he saw him, he had compassion. He went to him and bound up his wounds, pouring on oil and wine. Then he set him on his own animal and brought him to an inn and took care of him. And the next day he took out two denarii and gave them to the innkeeper, saying, 'Take care of him, and whatever more you spend, I will repay you when I come back.' Which of these three, do you think, proved to be a neighbor to the man who fell among the robbers?" He said, "The one who showed him mercy." And Jesus said to him, "You go, and do likewise."

Luke 10:30–37

In this profound parable, we can find four truths that can help us love our LGBT neighbors in ways that honor Jesus and the gospel and will create opportunities to share the good news of Jesus!

Love people

In the parable we find a man who has been robbed and beaten. He is probably a Jew, though Jesus doesn't tell us that explicitly. All he tells us is that he is a human being in desperate need. One of the major points of the story is that to please God we must care for the neighbor right in front of us, no matter who he or she is (or what they might have done). Our neighbors are not only people who are like us, but biblically speaking, they are the people we interact with throughout our normal day. For many of us, our neighbors are men and women who are immersed in a gay identity.

Like the Good Samaritan, we are called to do good to our neighbors when we find them in need. What would happen if, as we interact with our LGBT "neighbors," we sought ways to do them good? What if instead of fear, disdain, and arrogance, we humbly served them? What if churches became known for such kindness? We don't need to compromise the gospel; it is very possible to do good to those who are lost. It is possible to be nice and orthodox. Jesus did it all the time and so can we.

Do not let religion get in the way of loving your LGBT neighbors

The two religious men in this parable are not portrayed in a positive light. Both the priest and the Levite are men who have the right religion: They follow the God of Abraham. But the way they dogmatically carry out their religion keeps them from loving the injured man; they know that if the man is dead and they touch him, they would be ceremonially unclean. Therefore, they don't even get near enough to see if he is alive. Rather than paving the way for them to love others, their religion becomes an excuse and a barrier. They become bad examples of what it means to be a follower of God.

It has become a popular notion that Christians are known much more for what we are against than what we are for. In some ways, this is unavoidable. Certainly we want to make sure the integrity of Scripture is maintained, and we want to ensure that the gospel we proclaim is the one that Jesus proclaimed. So in a culture and a church that wants to redefine everything—right and wrong, marriage, the sanctity of life—we react. But let's make sure that our defense of Scripture and the gospel does not become an excuse not to love those with whom we strongly disagree.

When I began interacting with the church as a young adult, still immersed in sexual sin and darkness, I was, in every sense, unclean. I wasn't able to live in obscurity in a pew; my story followed me to church. Many people knew just what a mess I was. I came scared, alone, and in bondage. The church that I attended could have confronted me, disciplined me, and marginalized me. They did not. Instead, I was loved. I was accepted into the community. I was cared for. Their love, acceptance, and kindness opened up doors in my heart to receive the gospel. Their actions spoke loudly. They were the hands and feet of Jesus. This has always stuck with me. As a leader I have decided to make sure that the churches I am a part of are such communities. I don't want our religion to get in the way of being like Jesus. I pray you feel the same as well.

Acknowledge the good that your LGBT neighbors can do

The turning point in the story comes when Jesus introduces the hero. To the surprise of the audience, it is a Samaritan. Leon

Morris tells us, "The audience would have expected a priest and a Levite to be followed by an Israelite layman. They would almost certainly now be expecting a story with an anti-clerical twist."[3] Instead, a person every respectable Jew would detest is revealed as the hero. It is a despised Samaritan who does the right thing and shows compassion. It is a Samaritan who gets at God's heart for the injured neighbor.

We need to admit that there are Good Samaritans in the LGBT community. I am thankful for how many in the LGBT community have stood up against the use of hatred and violence against young men and women in conflict with their sexual identity. Bullying, hateful speech, and violence are not uncommon experiences for young men and women who think they might be gay.[4] The world can be cruel to those who are different.

The LGBT community is seeking ways to reduce these incidences. Of course, I absolutely don't agree with much that the political apparatus of the LGBT community does, but the protection of maturing young men and women from bullying and violence is good work. It is just like what the Samaritan did for the injured man. And we ought to celebrate it and even join them in helping end this cruelty.

A theology of doing good

The Good Samaritan gets involved. He bandages up the injured man, gets him to an inn so he can recover, and pays for it all. His compassion isn't just lip-service or a few hurried minutes of assistance; it is intentional care that takes time and resources. He gets involved in the life of the man in need. He doesn't worry about how it looks or his personal safety or what it will cost him. All he seems concerned about is making sure that the injured man gets well.

There is a demand in this story: To please God by loving our neighbor, we need to get radically involved in doing good to the people we encounter every day. One of the reasons many of us don't do this regularly is that we lack theological vision for such neighborly kindness. The sixteenth-century reformer John Calvin helps to give us such a vision. He writes,

> The Lord commands us to do good unto all men without exception though the majority are very undeserving when judged according to their own merits. But scripture here helps us out with an excellent argument when it teaches us that we must not think of man's real value, but only of his creation in the image of God to which we owe all possible honor and love.[5]

We can do good and be in relationship with our gay and lesbian friends because they are bearers of the image of God. So in a real sense, we are not doing good to them but to the God we dearly desire to honor. Our good is not acceptance of unbiblical lifestyles but the honoring of God's image in individuals.

Good Samaritan Evangelism

The story of the Good Samaritan seeks to teach us how to treat those we interact with on a daily basis. But I do think it can also help us with a strategy of evangelism as we face a skeptical, unbelieving gay community. I think it is true that people are more willing to hear our opinions when they truly think we care for them. I think the church would do well to be Good Samaritans to their gay and lesbian neighbors—doing good, acknowledging the good they do, being respectful, honoring the image of God, and entering into actual friendships. And when the moment presents itself, speak clearly the gospel of Jesus—grace, repentance, and obedience. This coupling of being good neighbors with the gospel is what I call Good Samaritan Evangelism.

As leaders, my wife and I have this as our vision of evangelism. We aren't good at it yet, but we want to be. We have had the honor of meeting and being in relationship with many men and women who have struggled with homosexuality. We have been in small groups together, we have had meals together, we have laughed together, we have had hard conversations together, and we have sought to honor the image of God in them. Our hope is that the gospel will be declared and many will say yes to Jesus.

Conclusion

The complicated issue of homosexuality threatens to tear the church apart. But God has other plans. This is another moment when his church can shine. Instead of being seen as insular and arrogant, we can follow Jesus. We can care more about people even when their lives are contrary to the gospel; we can make sure that our religion propels us to love; we can be unafraid of blessing the good that we see in the LGBT community; and finally, we can build real friendships with our LGBT neighbors. And when opportunity arises, we can share the hope that burns within us.

Takeaway

The latest sociological research concludes that many non-Christians believe the church is full of narrow-minded homophobes. Looking at the story of the Good Samaritan, we answered the question of how we as the church should treat and be in relationship with the gay community. Maybe the survey will look different a decade from now!

Here's the Church, Here's the Steeple

How should my church deal with this issue?

Dentist Drill - Novocain = Church Politics

We (Ron and Adam) have been serving together in a denomination that is in trouble. The Reformed Church in America is not just an organization. It is a set of friendships and ministry connections stretching back to before the United States was founded. Sadly, this web of community is being torn apart. In spite of numerous church statements on homosexuality, each one affirming the truths we have highlighted in this book, a growing number of our churches and leaders are promoting a pro-LGBT theology, including many pastors and professors at our colleges and seminaries.

Most of the time, we can do ministry in our local congregations without giving a second thought to these realities. We share the gospel, reach out to lost and broken people, and hold out the hope of transformation that is ours in Jesus. Most of the time.

Then there are the denominational gatherings. Leaders from churches around the country come together for a week of informational sharing, corporate worship, dialogue, and debate. It can be a great time of reunion with old friends and a chance to form new relationships.

At the same time, it is often an incredibly painful experience. Any illusions that "things really aren't that bad" are swept away as our real differences come to light once again. Arguments are made. Rainbow-flag pins abound. Interest groups gather, pray, and plan. In the end, there are a lot of politics. It is easy to be turned off. But the temptation to simply dismiss the whole debacle is misguided. This isn't just a debate over how we define a doctrine. In the end, our differences are producing diametrically opposed visions for gospel ministry.

Our denominational experience is really just one small manifestation of a fault line that is forming in the church.

The Ground Is Starting to Shake

On Good Friday 1964, the greatest earthquake in American history shook Alaska, fracturing streets, shattering buildings, and unleashing tsunamis that rocked the coastline. Some areas of land were thrust high into the sky, others plummeted. In three minutes, this magnitude 9.2 quake tipped a domino rally of destruction that led to 131 deaths.[1] It could have been much worse, but the population density in Alaska isn't like that of the East Coast.

Imagine waking up to the quake. Imagine a fault line running through the middle of town, dividing one section from another. One set of buildings rushes thirty feet into the air. Another set drops by eight. The whole thing would seem like a random, sudden rush of events. But earthquakes don't happen suddenly. They build for decades, centuries, millennia. As plates in the earth's crust slowly move against each other, pressure builds. Eventually, that pressure exceeds the strength of the rock, snapping it like a rubber band pulled too far. Our experience of the earthquake is really just the last straw of a geological process that was taking place far beneath our great-great-grandmother's kitchen table.

The church in America is moving through a season of division. You might be in a denomination that has clear statements. You might be in a nondenominational church where everyone agrees. You might think this issue is just something "out there." But the kind of debates we have been having in our denominational gatherings will soon be working their way down to local congregations. We might experience different degrees of engagement with the issue, but the reality is the same: Over the next five to ten years, the American church will move through a "sorting." Every pastor and local congregation will have to engage this issue and deal with it.

There are two ways to respond to challenging situations. The first is to be reactive. Here is a reactive response: You're on a long road trip, when suddenly the oil light comes on. Because you didn't check the oil at the last rest stop, you now have to deal with a breakdown on the highway. When we're in reaction mode, we are usually surprised. We are rushing to deal with a pressing problem. Often, this means dropping whatever we're doing, running over anyone in our path, and learning from our mistakes about how *not* to do something.

The other way to handle difficult situations is to be proactive. Proactive people take a look at where things are headed and do their best to plan accordingly. "Hope for the best; plan for the worst" is the motto of the proactive person. If we knew the earthquake was coming, we could do something to prepare for it.

The Question Behind the Questions

At the heart of this chapter is a basic question: *If the local church is called to be a holy community of saved sinners, then how do we integrate and minister to sexually broken people?* How can we both welcome people into our community and clearly distinguish what it means to be a member? Our local churches should be manifestations of God's kingdom in a dark world. Hopefully, church members possess genuine faith. That means we have confessed our sins, embraced the gospel, and are seeking to shape our entire identity around God's vision for our lives. In other words, it means committed, sometimes messy, discipleship.

In our "everyone's welcome" world, the local church can easily become a collection of people who simply enjoy hanging out together, doing nice things, and singing happy songs. On the other hand, in our increasingly confused and debauched world, local churches can easily become defensive, reactionary fortresses that exclude anyone with obvious "issues."

This chapter is our effort to inspire proactive responses in local churches. It is not a collection of cookie-cutter solutions to every possible scenario, but we hope it will lead churches to begin discussing ways to handle the tensions that will arise as we bring gospel ministry to a culture in upheaval.

Questions and Answers

How should our church outline the relational choices for a follower of Jesus who struggles with same-sex desire?

Every Christian is commanded to live a life of sexual purity. The only valid expression of sexuality is in the bonds of marriage—one man, one woman, for life (1 Corinthians 7). Every other sexual expression is sinful. For someone struggling with same-sex desire, this biblical boundary offers two valid choices: celibacy/singleness or heterosexual marriage.

For some who deal with homosexual desire, singleness will be their choice. They will take the energy, time, and resources that a good marriage demands and give them to the Lord as an offering. This of course comes with relational suffering. Humans are meant to be in intimate relationship. When this does not happen, a great void is left. Nevertheless, singles can have forms of relational intimacy that are not sexual. Thankfully, there are beautiful examples of men and women who are living this well. Sam Allberry is one such example—an Anglican pastor, writer, and someone who loves God, takes seriously his Scripture, and lives out the demands of it through a single life.[2]

For others, heterosexual marriage is a real choice. One of the sad obstacles to marriage for some who deal with same-sex attraction is the fear that they won't have strong sexual feelings for their opposite-sex spouse. Sexual attraction is important, but I (Ron) can tell you that it comes and goes in marriage even among heterosexuals! Marriage is more than sex. You can be attracted to your spouse and still be struggling with same-sex attraction. Christian marriage is about companionship, stability, lifelong friendship, financial security, and providing an environment in which children can grow and thrive. Of course, sexuality is an essential component. A couple can have sexual intimacy even if one is struggling with same-sex issues. For sure, one should not bring ongoing sexual sin and darkness into a marriage, but if both a husband and wife enter into the covenant with their eyes wide open, there is no reason that the marriage cannot be a long-lasting, joyful union.

A member of our church is trying to get a petition together that will ask our local school district to ban the Gay-Straight Alliance club that has formed in the high school. This church member is passing the petition around in the church lobby before and after services and has asked us to post it on our bulletin board. What should we do?

Parents have reasons to be concerned about these groups.[3] GSAs guide students to explore and define their sexuality, often without a parent's knowledge. They promote an unbiblical perspective of human sexuality and may even connect students with "open and affirming" religious leaders who convince them that their church is "homophobic." GSAs help define school culture, creating a climate where students who do not show support can be marginalized.

Understandably, many church members would want to stop a GSA from forming. However, the church foyer is probably not the best place to organize resistance. Why? First, because Christians who agree on biblical sexuality might have honest disagreement about the way we should be active in our community. The gospel ministry of the local church and the civic engagement of the individual believer are not one and the same. Second, by supporting this petition, the church might inadvertently be supporting the removal of *all* clubs. For instance, it might be legally impossible to shut down the GSA without also closing the Fellowship of Christian Athletes. Finally, it would be *way* too easy for a first-time visitor to view this public petition drive as a signal that they are unwelcome.

If you feel called to "do something," consider asking your pastor to hold an informational meeting where people can learn and ask questions. Invite a school official in for conversation. Also, encourage the Christian students in your school to take advantage of any avenues for forming a group that promotes biblically faithful sexuality.

A gay couple has been bringing their child to our midweek children's programming. They've indicated that they'd like to be able to help out with the program. What do we do?

First of all, how wonderful that a gay couple is coming to your church! This is no small thing. God is drawing them by his grace. Hopefully, friendships have been formed, community is being lived out, and this conversation can happen in the context of relationships. A couple of things to consider:

1. Does your church have a policy concerning who can serve in your children's programming? If so, does the policy include a standard-of-living requirement (i.e., one's life will be congruent with a Christian witness)? If your church requires that a person serving the children have a life that reflects a Christian commitment, then it's time to have a hard conversation. This can be done humbly and graciously. But it needs to be done.

If no such requirement exists, then

2. How do they want to serve? Do they want to lead the lessons? Or help with refreshments? Do they want to serve together? There is a difference between leading and serving/assisting. Leadership requires a certain level of Christian maturity. If someone wants to lead children they need to be on the journey of discipleship; they need a life that you would want your child to emulate. It sounds like this couple is still together, so it would prohibit them from leading. But they might be able to serve. Maybe helping set up chairs and the area before a lesson or cleaning up afterwards. Either way, at some point, you will have to have the awkward, hard conversation. Their relationship is contrary to the gospel. Explain that though they are welcome

to be a part of your community, some opportunities to lead and serve will be closed to them.

A same-sex couple who has been coming to our church on and off over the last year heard about our church's marriage retreat and signed up. I'm on the marriage retreat committee and don't know what to do. We discussed the matter and learned that this couple was legally married last year. How do we handle this?

First, we suggest you enlist the help of your pastor, a church staff member, and/or elder in handling this kind of situation. It will have a significant impact on the couple and your congregation, potentially involving your church in a public firestorm. Hopefully your church has a statement on the biblical definition of marriage. Such a statement will certainly help.

Initially, the approach to such a couple is fairly straightforward. They should be lovingly informed that the church's perspective on marriage is one man, one woman in an exclusive, lifetime covenant. That definition of marriage determines who should or shouldn't come to your annual marriage retreat. For instance, a cohabiting, unmarried couple would not be allowed to come. A man and woman would not be able to leave their spouses for the weekend to come to the retreat together. Handled carefully, this circumstance would open the door for you to have an honest, open conversation about the Bible's message on human sexuality. It might even open the door for them to consider the claims of the gospel on their own lives.

We should not miss the broader concerns implied in this question. As our culture increasingly recognizes same-sex marriage (and "family" in myriad other forms), we will need to have clear guidance and policy. Local churches without such statements run the risk of appearing arbitrary in their decision making and may even open themselves to legal difficulties.

Should practicing homosexuals or homosexuals in a committed relationship be allowed to join a congregation?

In a day when many churches have abandoned the concept of "membership," we believe it is more important than ever to have a clear and well-communicated process for joining. Church membership helps people understand that saving faith is confirmed not only by an internal feeling but also by a certain set of convictions and even the witness of the church. By joining a church, members are opening their lives to the spiritual guidance of recognized leaders, welcoming their support, exhortation, and even spiritual correction.

Far from creating an insiders vs. outsiders club, a well-defined membership process allows people to consider the claims of true gospel-centered community. Questions like this one will be brought to light as a class walks through the belief statements of the church. In the same way we would deal with other areas of open, unrepentant sin (e.g., a man and woman in an adulterous relationship), we should find a sensitive way to address this question.

The short answer would be something like "Joining our church means making a public profession that Jesus is the Lord of your life. That means you have determined to obey him and trust his Word. While every person in our congregation is a struggling sinner, we seek to submit to Scripture and agree to hold each other accountable. This area of unrepentant sin would indicate you're not ready to join us in that shared commitment. Let's keep talking and working through this together."

I am a pastor or leader in the church who must interact with other leaders (either in my denomination or other churches) who disagree with me on the issue of homosexuality; how should I treat those who disagree with me?

First of all, be pleasant. If we are right, then we ought to be able to be with those with whom we disagree without getting defensive. These leaders are made in the image of God, and you can be kind. Second, be humble. Being right doesn't mean you can be an arrogant jerk. I have seen many friends come across as unfriendly and cocky. They lose the battle because they lack expression of the character of Christ. So find ways to soften your approach. Be friendly. Third, speak the truth. As well as you are able, when appropriate, declare the Scriptures and what they have to say. There is no need to hide the truth of the gospel. Those who disagree with you are freely sharing their opinion; you have the same right. Just be smart, kind, and humble. Finally, pray! Pray that God will soften their hearts and lead them to repentance. Pray that they won't deceive those they lead, and pray that God, in Christ, will be glorified in your interactions. And pray that God will give you the strength to be a kind, humble proclaimer of his good gospel.

Are the leaders at "open and affirming" churches truly Christians? Second John 1:9 says, "Everyone who goes on ahead and does not abide in the teaching of Christ, does not have God." I really wrestle with how to deal with people who bear the name brother or sister and yet do such things.

The church's perennial struggle is not with society, which has always been confused about sex. It is not with believers who may be questioning their own sexuality; we have always been sinners seeking holiness. Our true struggle is with the rising volume of false voices that claim to be teachers of the gospel. A massive amount of the New Testament warns against false teachers—those who claim the name of Christ but actually lead people away from him:

- Jesus makes it clear: "Whoever causes one of these little ones who believe in me to sin, it would be better for him if a great millstone were hung around his neck and he were thrown into the sea" (Mark 9:42).
- Paul puts it bluntly: "If anyone teaches a different doctrine and does not agree with the sound words of our Lord Jesus Christ and the teaching that accords with godliness, he is puffed up with conceit and understands nothing" (1 Timothy 6:3–4).
- Peter promises, "There will be false teachers among you, who will secretly bring in destructive heresies, even denying the Master who bought them, bringing upon themselves swift destruction" (2 Peter 2:1).
- Jude warns that teachers promoting sexual immorality are destined for "the gloom of utter darkness" (Jude 1:13).

We believe that church leaders promoting a revisionist gospel fall into the New Testament category of "false teachers." These teachers, meant to lead people to Jesus, are instead drawing souls away from the cross. To the extent that they deny a biblical definition of sin, they have abandoned the authentic proclamation of the gospel. By rejecting the Word of Christ, they are betraying his lordship. In the end, they teach that we can have true faith without genuine repentance and submission. The end result: Many people are being led astray.

We write these things with tears for those souls who have been deceived and denied the pure preaching of the Word. We pray that these teachers, some of whom we've counted friends, will turn in repentance. While only God can ultimately judge another person's eternal salvation, Scripture tells us how we should treat false teachers:

> Everyone who goes on ahead and does not abide in the teaching of Christ, does not have God. Whoever abides in the teaching has both the Father and the Son. If anyone comes to you and does not bring this teaching, do not receive him into your house or give him any greeting, for whoever greets him takes part in his wicked works.
>
> 2 John 1:9–11

Along with this strong affirmation of Scripture's teaching about false teachers, we want to add a word of caution: In a world with such confusing signals and with competing authorities, each claiming to have the "truth" on this issue, we should expect that good people may stray from Scripture. Some may even be leaders in the church. When a personal relationship affords the opportunity, we strongly suggest pursuing a course similar to Matthew 18:15–17 with a friend or leader who has adopted an unbiblical stance on this issue. Perhaps that person has been led astray and, like the lost sheep, can be brought back into the fold. False belief and teaching, like any other sin, can be repented of, and restoration is possible!

Do you think churches are going to be forced to perform same-sex weddings in the future?

Historically in the United States, thankfully, the church does enjoy immense freedom and protection. For now, our freedom to practice our religion according to conscience has been strongly protected. This includes churches' freedom not to perform same-sex weddings. Hopefully, this freedom and protection will not change. But the world is changing, and this could change as well. Already, businesses are being forced to do things against their moral conscience. If the cultural and political tides in the United States do not change, the church might be pressured to act contrary to its conscience. If this were to happen, hard decisions would have to be made.

In such a world, pastors and churches would have to defy the state and take a stand. What other choice would the church and its leaders have? If this were to happen, churches might lose tax benefits, pastors might be sued, and Christians might be pushed even farther to the margins. In such a world, everything would change. This shouldn't cause too much anxiety, though. This is our Father's world, and if such a shift should happen, then it must be for his purposes. He will use it for our good, for the pursuit of those he loves, and most of all for his glory and fame.

In this chapter, we have answered questions about what a biblically faithful local church should look like in a world filled with sexually confused people. We want to be a community of believers that confesses Jesus as Lord and lives as an authentic witness in the world while welcoming many to come, hear, belong, and believe in the good news of the gospel.

8

Spots on the Leopard

Can the gospel transform someone's sexual orientation?

Two years ago I (Ron) was at the inaugural conference of the Restored Hope Network (RHN). One hundred leaders gathered to start a network of churches and ministries dedicated to the hope of the gospel for men and women struggling with homosexuality.

Their stated purpose is to be "dedicated to restoring hope to those broken by sexual and relational sin, especially those impacted by homosexuality. We proclaim that Jesus Christ has life-changing power for all who submit to Christ as Lord."[1]

Many friends were present who have been transformed in their sexuality by the power of the gospel: Andrew Comiskey—former homosexual, now Catholic theologian—was there. He offers a powerful prophetic voice to the church that the gospel can transform anyone; he is married and has four adult children. He is a good friend and one of the first leaders who saw God's calling on my life. He was instrumental in my transformation, and I am thankful for his good ministry. Anne Paulk, a former lesbian, has walked for decades in the powerful reality of Christ's transformation. Dean Greer—a formerly gay man who contracted HIV in the lifestyle—is now living radically for Jesus, is married, and is the father of a beautiful son. These are just three among the countless stories of transformation and grace. As these amazing leaders shared their lives and proclaimed the good news of the gospel, I was reminded that in Jesus there really is good news. The gospel does change lives.

When I came to Jesus, my sexuality was in disarray. I had strong heterosexual feelings and strong homosexual feelings, all of it exaggerated. If I had to categorize myself, I'd use the term *bisexual*. I had had numerous sexual experiences, I was addicted to pornography, and I had broken through various biblical sexual boundaries. All that remained was a catastrophe. This is where Jesus met me.

Over the next five years, I was immersed in his community and his life. And during that time, I found radical transformation. As someone who has followed Jesus for seventeen years, has been a pastor for ten, and as someone who has seen countless men and women work out their salvation as it relates to their broken sexuality, *I know* that Jesus promises radical transformation for the sexual sinner.

I also know that these are controversial words these days both in our world and in the church. Some men and women have not experienced a consistent change in their sexual orientation, yet love Jesus and truly desire to follow him faithfully. According to their own testimony, they seek to submit their lives and bodies to God's plan for sexuality, yet they experience same-sex orientation. It would be disrespectful to denounce the experience of these believers as untrue. It would be dishonoring to the Holy Spirit's work to assume their continued struggle indicates some form of "second-class" Christianity.

But we can acknowledge some people's experience without falling into the opposite extreme: denying that the gospel transforms. Today, even mentioning the idea of transformation is labeled as ridiculous. Our culture has reduced this question of transformation to a silly slogan: "Pray the gay away." California and New Jersey are leading the way to make sure that therapists cannot help a person seeking to manage and change unwanted sexual desires. There is a strong wave of political correctness that is seeking to bar men and women, especially the young, from living out the biblical demands concerning their sexuality.[2]

The world, and even some in the church, has declared that the gospel has little to offer to the same-sex struggler. The question of whether a person can change his or her sexuality is a complex and significant issue, and I don't pretend to have all the answers. But I do think the church as a whole is forgetting the transforming power found in the person and work of Jesus.

What follows is not a critique, nor am I trying to over promise what the gospel might accomplish. Instead, I would like the church not to lose what has always been true: The gospel of Jesus is good news to those who struggle with same-sex desire. This chapter is included as an apologetic of transformation.

Let's Get Our Definitions Straight

"I was born this way" is the common refrain when talking about homosexuality these days. The very statement is meant to end debates, hush questions, and engender understanding and mercy in the hearers. Who can argue with such a truth claim, if it is true? But does this simplistic, one-dimensional account of human sexuality really make sense? Are people simply born with a sexual identity, bound to live in it their entire lives?

If our discourse is bound by the narrow vocabulary of conventional wisdom, then we will be cut off from describing the biblical reality of transformation. Unless we can broaden the range of perspective, we will be talking past each other as we engage our culture. This should not stop us from having the conversation. Instead, we must speak carefully. This careful speaking will help us when we come to the hard questions of transformation. Mark Yarhouse, in his excellent book *Homosexuality and the Christian*, offers some of the best sociological insights on the nature of sexual orientation, identity, and desire. These insights are foundational in answering the question of whether or not the gospel can transform our sexuality.

Desire

Think about the attractions you have. They are innate, they bubble up from your body. They are not a choice. For most people, sexual desire results in attraction to the opposite sex. They do not choose this desire, it just is. People who have same-sex desires are not choosing them. The desires simply exist in their bodies. They are physical. Yarhouse writes, "Certain people, regardless of the cause, have experiences of attraction to the same sex. . . . [This] is descriptive. We are simply talking about the fact that a person experiences same-sex attraction."[3] This is what we mean when we refer to same-sex desire.

Orientation

Orientation is the spectrum by which we experience our sexual desire. Yarhouse writes, "When people talk about having a homosexual orientation, they are essentially saying that they experience a same-sex attraction that is strong enough, durable enough, and persistent enough for them to feel that they are *oriented* toward the same sex."[4] Someone with a homosexual orientation is a man or woman who experiences homosexual desire to such a degree that their sexual orientation points only toward the same sex.

Sexual identity

Sexual identity is a subjective, fairly modern cultural label. Yarhouse writes,

> Although homosexual behavior has been practiced in other cultures throughout history, we are the first culture in which people refer to themselves in this way. There was never a language for it, and there has never been community support for this kind of identification or labeling. Until recently, there was not even a way to say it.[5]

Today in our culture, we find a don't-overthink-it assumption that a person with a homosexual orientation must embrace a gay identity if he or she is to be true to himself or herself. The thinking goes: If you feel it, it must be real and exalted as the primary reality of your identity.

Sexual behavior

Sexual behavior is acting out one's desire. It is the final step of a complex mixture of desire, orientation, and identity. We make choices about our behavior based upon who we are and who we desire to be. Behavior is the objective marker of who a person is. In a very real sense, I am what I do.

Is Transformation Possible?

Keeping these helpful definitions in mind, we can start asking the questions that are answerable. Can the gospel transform a person's desires? A person's orientation? A person's identity? A person's behavior? Hear these stunning words from Paul:

> Or do you not know that the unrighteous will not inherit the kingdom of God? Do not be deceived: neither the sexually immoral, nor idolaters, nor adulterers, nor men who practice

homosexuality, nor thieves, nor the greedy, nor drunkards, nor revilers, nor swindlers will inherit the kingdom of God. And such were some of you. But you were washed, you were sanctified, you were justified in the name of the Lord Jesus Christ and by the Spirit of our God.

1 Corinthians 6:9–11

The Corinthian church was a wild bunch. They experienced sexual scandals, they had worldly values, and when they got into fights, they were known to take their Christian brothers or sisters to court! So here, Paul is seeking to get the Corinthian church on the right track. And here, as clearly as can be seen, Paul helps us answer the fundamental questions of whether transformation is possible, and if so, what it looks like.

Transformed identity—"such were some of you"

Paul reminds members of the church in Corinth of who they used to be: "Such were some of you." Apparently, some members of the community in Corinth were former thieves, homosexuals, drunks, and swindlers. They were quite a church (one that I think I would have felt right at home in!). This is who they *used* to be. Now they have a new identification; they live in a new reality.

This new identity isn't oriented around a sex act, or any other particular sin activity, but around the reality of God's grace: "You were washed." This great community of men and women in Corinth was immersed in the atoning mercy found in Jesus, and they were clean. There seems little doubt that the church in Corinth would have automatically heard this "washing" as an allusion to baptism.

Baptism is the act that signifies a new identity, one centered in the Father, Son, and Spirit. When Jesus told his disciples in

Matthew 28 to baptize in the name of the Trinitarian God, he wasn't just mouthing a slogan to be spoken like magic over the one being baptized. Instead, it was the proclamation of a new reality. The person baptized was being brought into a new family, a new community. This was now their primary identity.

For any follower of Jesus, our identity is in God himself, specifically the person and work of Jesus Christ. We are no longer the sum of our actions, desires, biological inclinations, or cultural pressures. We are his. This is true for everyone, even gay and lesbian strugglers. *So we can say clearly, without equivocation, that the gospel can change one's identity.* As a matter of fact, this is precisely what the gospel does! Someone can be gay before meeting Jesus, having her whole life centered on her fractured sexuality; and then after finding Jesus, her identity can be centered on Christ. Notice something important: The goal of the gospel's transformation is not healthy heterosexuality. *It is total identification with Christ.* This is what the gospel can do for a person's identity.

Transformed behavior

Paul reminds the Corinthian church of the transformation possible in Jesus and his kingdom. In chapter 5 of 1 Corinthians, Paul lambasts the church because of their permissiveness as it relates to gross sexual sin. In chapter 6, he makes clear that those who center their lives on sexual sin will not inherit the kingdom of God. Paul is seeking to stir the Christian passions of his hearers.

Instead of permitting sexual sin, Paul calls the sexual sinner into the same redemptive story that others in Corinth had experienced. Instead of cheap grace (a grace that says anything goes because Jesus has paid the price), Paul invites the sexual sinner into biblical grace—one that demands repentance. He does all of this by reminding them of the reality they all face:

judgment. *"Or do you not know that the unrighteous will not inherit the kingdom of God?"* Without changed behavior, there can be no assurance of salvation. A basic, underlying assumption for Paul is that the demand of the gospel can be fulfilled through the sanctification of walking with Jesus.

Can a person imprisoned in the passions of a homosexual lifestyle find purity? There seems little doubt that Paul would answer YES! The power of Christ and his cross has the ability to change our depraved behavior. This is hard work for sure, bloody in fact. It is not easy to die to one's old passions. But the cross makes a way. Power is available for anyone who cries out to Jesus. Will there be suffering? Pain? Anguish? Yes! But make no mistake, there *will* be change.

Transformed desires

Can the gospel of Jesus change our attractions? Can a person struggling with homosexuality know with certainty that the gospel promises a change in desire? Of course, anyone who has same-sex desire and seeks to faithfully follow Jesus hopes the desire will go away. To walk with such a limp in this life is hard. I know. For some, including me, there will be significant change in desire. I have strong sexual desire for my wife. Praise God! This is a gift for which I am thankful.

But many will have to manage their same-sex desire in community and before Jesus. Nowhere in Scripture, and specifically nowhere in 1 Corinthians, does God promise that we will not be tempted with the old, dead things. We all have crosses to bear. And those of us whose cross is our homosexual desire can't become victims just because ours is unique. Paul is right:

No temptation has overtaken you that is not common to man. God is faithful, and he will not let you be tempted beyond your ability, but with the temptation he will also provide the way of escape, that you may be able to endure it.

1 Corinthians 10:13

We are offered enough grace for this life, no matter the struggle

To be honest, we will each make progress in this life to varying degrees. Some of us, full of holy intention and desire, will stumble through life taking two steps forward and one step back, but even that is the pathway to transformation:

> But if you are a poor creature—poisoned by a wretched upbringing in some house full of vulgar jealousies and senseless quarrels—saddled, by no choice of your own, with some loathsome sexual perversion—nagged day in and day out by an inferiority complex that makes you snap at your best friends—do not despair. He knows all about it. You are one of the poor whom He blessed. He knows what a wretched machine you are trying to drive. Keep on. Do what you can. One day . . . He will fling it on the scrap-heap and give you a new one. And then you may astonish us all—not least yourself.[6]

A day will come when the old aches and hungers are gone. There will be a day when all is made new and we will be fully whole. Some of us will begin to see this newness in this life. But even if we struggle with old desires, we need not despair. It may be night, but morning is coming.

The Journey of Transformation

I have many talents, but one of them is not a good sense of direction. I get lost all the time. I have gotten lost going to work from my house. One of the best tools I have is my GPS. I use it all the time because it helps me go where I need to go. I have found that I need the same directional leadership when it comes to walking out transformation in my life.

The Bible promises transformation. Though this is a theological reality, it can be difficult to actually get there in real life. What follows are GPS markers that have helped innumerable people find transformation. They are laid out here to show just how practical and real transformation is. Again, this is important, because if the path isn't clear, simple, and proven, it can be hard to offer it humbly.

GPS marker #1—See the Son!

You were washed, you were sanctified, you were justified in the name of the Lord Jesus Christ and by the Spirit of our God.

1 Corinthians 6:11

Seventeen years ago, I was broken, sinful, and desperate. I had said yes to Jesus' offer of life, but life and hope seemed bleak. My same-sex passions were still strong. I was so hungry. My soul was broken—sexually confused, damaged from the many sexual partners, alone, addicted to porn—and my mind was under the bondage of lust. It was there, in profound darkness, that I met Jesus. This is why I love him so much. I remember those early days just spending hours worshiping him in my little room. I remember being so hungry for his presence. Real transformation happens in the reality of the Father, Son, and Spirit. St. Augustine, a sexual deviant just like me, who was touched by the great grace of God, writes this:

Those who want to find their joy in externals all too easily grow empty themselves. They pour themselves out on things which, being seen, are but transient, and lick even the images of these things with their famished imagination. If only they would weary of their starvation and ask, *Who will show us good things?* Let us answer them, and let them hear the truth: *The light of your countenance has set its seal upon us, O Lord....* Ah, if only they could see the eternal reality within![7]

This is true. If the same-sex struggler feeds on the petty, miserable, dark same-sex identity, desire, and sin, there will be no change. But if he sees Jesus—spends time with him, falls in love with him, and learns from him—transformation will most certainly happen. The reality of Jesus and his ability to raise our affections is beyond description. This does not mean that a same-sex struggler will no longer have same-sex feelings; it means that those feelings will get swallowed up in the greater affection he has for God. A flashlight is powerful in a dark room, but it is worthless in the glare of the noonday sun. Homosexual desire is powerful in the darkness of sin and death. But it is simply powerless in the light of the Son.

The hope for the sexual sinner is not a psychological breakthrough or great cognitive behavioral therapy, or even Christian practices. The great hope for the sexual sinner, what will begin to set things right, is to catch a glimpse of Jesus.

To catch a glimpse of Jesus is to simply delight in who he is. This is what we are made for. Sam Storms writes,

> You weren't created for boredom or burnout or bondage to sexual lust or greed or ambition but for the incomparable pleasure and matchless joy that knowing Jesus alone can bring. Only then, in him, will you encounter the life-changing, thirst-quenching, soul-satisfying delight that God, for his glory, created you to experience.[8]

I have experienced this many times, such as in reading and praying the Psalms, thinking about what they mean to me. I have experienced this in Sunday morning worship—his presence that sustains and feeds my soul. I experience this in Christian friendships that give me life and help me live the life I desire. Truthfully, as I seek the Lord, I find him, and it has made all the difference.

GPS marker #2—Self-denial

Or do you not know that the unrighteous will not inherit the kingdom of God? Do not be deceived.

1 Corinthians 6:9

There is no doubt that having our eyes set on Jesus, actually experiencing the life he offers, is primary in our transformation. Jesus is foundational, but we must respond. The "unrighteous" in verse 9 are those who live just like the world. Paul wants to make sure that the Corinthian church is not deceived: Just believing in Jesus with intellectual assent is not enough. There must be repentance. There must be rejection of sin and its acts.

A false idea is floating about the church today hinting that we can enjoy the kindness of Jesus without obeying his clear commands. Nothing could be further from the truth. We must repent. John Calvin writes,

> The service of the Lord does not only include implicit obedience, but also a willingness to put aside our sinful desires, and to surrender completely to the leadership of the Holy Spirit.[9]

Transformation for the same-sex struggler happens when he or she is willing to be obedient.

This is painful. In Colossians, Paul writes, "Put to death therefore what is earthly in you" (3:5). For those who have embraced sexual sin, when you seek to wean the body from the addictive fix of sexual gratification, it screams. I know. But you cannot have the life he offers if you are not willing to repent and be obedient.

We enter into repentance and obedience through self-denial. Again, Calvin writes,

> It is an ancient and true observation that there is a world of vices hidden in the soul of man, but Christian self-denial is the remedy of them all. There is deliverance in store only for the man who gives up his selfishness, and whose sole aim is to please the Lord and to do what is right in his sight.[10]

Paul helps the Corinthians put this in context: For those who embrace unrighteousness, there will be no kingdom of God. But for those who put their flesh to death, the opposite is true. There will be a day when the suffering, pain, agony, and obedience will be worth it. We will be with him. This is the transformation he offers the same-sex struggler.

GPS marker #3—The church

Paul is writing to a church! These sexual sinners in Corinth who had experienced radical transformation realized such life change in a local community. I am the man I am today because I have decided to work out my salvation in and through the local church. This means bringing honesty and confession, and in return receiving comfort, correction, and encouragement. Men and women who struggle with same-sex desire and who desire real transformation must be firmly planted in a local church that is mature and prepared to walk with those who are seeking transformation. This journey out of the bondage of homosexual sin is hard enough. It's next to impossible on your own.

One of the great comforts of the church is that it reminds us of the objective grace and love of Jesus. Dietrich Bonhoeffer writes,

In the presence of a psychiatrist I can only be a sick man; in the presence of a Christian brother I can dare to be a sinner. The psychiatrist must first search my heart and yet he never plumbs its ultimate depth. The Christian brother knows when I come to him: here is a sinner like myself, a godless man who wants to confess and yearns for God's forgiveness. The psychiatrist views me as if there were no God. The brother views me as I am before the judging and merciful God in the Cross of Jesus Christ.[11]

In the church, we encounter the living Christ—his mercy and his judgment. Transformation, then, is with other brothers and sisters who are also seeking to be obedient to Jesus. I have seen this play out powerfully in small-group recovery ministries run in the local church. Using curriculum from ministries like Celebrate Recovery or Desert Stream,[12] these small groups provide the spaces where men and women can work out their salvation. If a church is serious about standing for the truth of Scripture as it relates to sexuality, it must provide spaces for people to become the kinds of people who can live out the demands of the gospel. Otherwise, our gospel stand sounds like one more thing we are against. God desires to do much more.

The Change Is Real

You were washed, you were sanctified, you were justified in the name of the Lord Jesus Christ and by the Spirit of our God.

1 Corinthians 6:11

Paul reminds those Corinthians who had actually experienced a life change how it happened. It wasn't their effort that made it happen. It wasn't ecstatic religious experiences that made it happen. It wasn't some psychological insight that made it happen. Instead, the cross of Christ was the means of radical transformation. What was true for the Corinthian church is true for the same-sex struggler. The real work of transformation has already been done.

Through the cross, Jesus washes the same-sex struggler. The stain of shame that I felt as a man who had same-sex feelings and who had acted out was deep and wide. There were run-of-the-mill sinners, and then there was me. For me, same-sex sin was like a disease that had deep roots in my heart. And in those early days, months, and years of following Jesus, my soul reeked of shame. But in Jesus, I was washed. This happened. Paul reminds the Corinthian church that this is what the cross does. The cross of Jesus washes those who submit to him as Lord. We can be clean! The stain of sexual sin need not stay with us. What a relief.

Through the cross, the same-sex struggler—like all sinners—is justified. Same-sex sinners deserve the great wrath of God. They deserve not to inherit the kingdom of God. Their sin is foul. It deserves hell. I know. I have felt the condemnation of judgment that I rightly deserve because of my sin. Thank goodness for Jesus. Those who say yes to him find out that he has already said yes to them. The wrath of God is satisfied not by our moral efforts but by the Lamb of God slain.

The cross of Jesus sanctifies us. In 1 Corinthians 6:9–11, Paul is speaking of the dramatic ability of the act of Jesus' sacrifice to fully change a person. In one sense, he is speaking of that moment when we will die and be fully changed into the image of the Son. In another sense, he is speaking of what we will experience in this life, slowly but surely as Christ has his way in us. And finally, he is reminding the Corinthians of the real change they had already experienced. All of this is true for the same-sex struggler as well. There will be a day when all the suffering, longing, pain, doubt, and sin will vanish and we will be fully what we were meant to be.

Even in this life we can experience this transformation to some degree. Some of us will see our very desire change. For others, desires will still be marked by sin, but we will have our eyes on him and not give in to the impulses of sin and death. Those who follow Jesus and who struggle with same-sex desire can look back and see just how good he is. Remember how gracious he has been and what he has done for you.

Both the church and the culture are confused on whether the gospel offers hope to the same-sex struggler. Before we can answer such a question, we need to make sure we are using the same language. Otherwise, it is easy to just talk past each other. Jesus promises transformation of behavior and identity, and his claims are clear in Scripture. Even if unwanted desires remain, there is hope. The Scriptures offer a path of transformation that is knowable, simple, and clear. Countless Christians have walked it and reaped the benefits of it. What is experienced on this journey is real.

9

When Push Comes to Shove

How can we navigate the soon-to-be-everyday issues of living in a gay world?

Remember high school chemistry? In the cobwebby corridors of memory, we recall it worked something like this: There was the classroom portion, where you focused on theory. Then there was a lab section, where theory met practice. That was where things could get fun. (Any equation that includes teenagers, chemicals, and a Bunsen burner must have at least one possible outcome that reads: explosion.)

Our hope is that the chapters we have provided so far will give you a sense of the "theory" side of things. They lay out what we believe are good reasons for believing certain things and not others. Using Scripture as our basis, we have made the case that the gospel provides the way forward in a culture very confused on the issue of sexual intimacy. Our sexual sin— whether homosexual or heterosexual in nature—leads us out of the garden of God's blessing and into a wasteland. The gospel provides a way back.

We believe that people who receive and believe this message will be the opposite of judgmental jerks. We will be people who are acutely aware of our own need for forgiveness and gospel transformation. We will be able to have deep compassion. At the same time, we will not want to compromise with any ideology that threatens to short-circuit the gospel. To the extent that a philosophy soft-pedals our sin or tries to redefine what Scripture calls unrighteousness, that philosophy is withholding true freedom and forgiveness. The good news is not "Jesus likes us just the way we are." It is "Jesus died so that we could live a whole new life."

Hopefully, you have found these basic teachings convincing and helpful as you think through this tough topic. In this chapter, we want to offer some help with the more practical "lab" side of things. It is one thing to know what we believe; it is something else entirely to live it out. When push comes to shove, how will we live in the new normal? In our personal lives, how can we really embody compassion without compromise?

Questions and Answers: Compassion Without Compromise in Action

In preparing this chapter, we collected questions from a lot of people. We have way too many to cover in one chapter. Some of them arise from people's own experience. Some are hypothetical "What if?" queries that set up scenarios any of us would find daunting. Like you, we are learning the complex balancing act of reaching out in love, speaking truth with compassion, opening the doors for the gospel, and trying to be a good friend or family member. What does that look like in the context of our work, home, and social world?

We decided to list many of the questions we received, providing a glimpse of the diverse concerns expressed. We will only answer a few here, but we encourage you to check out the online resources connected with our book at www.Compassion WithoutCompromise.com. There, we will increasingly provide written and video responses to some of the other questions.

Something important to remember as you read through these: Real-life people stand behind each of these questions. Relationships. Personal stories. By necessity, we are keeping these answers brief and to the point. Though we are addressing "issues," we should never reduce real-life people to "problems" for us to solve. Each of these questions and answers needs to be worked out in a Spirit-led context of relationship.

How can I have a meaningful conversation about this issue without getting into an argument? How can I turn an argument into a meaningful conversation?

Paul was no stranger to difficult conversations. Sometimes, they ended with incredible conversions. Sometimes, they ended with his being stoned! His words to the Colossian church are relevant:

> [P]ray also for us, that God may open to us a door for the word, to declare the mystery of Christ, on account of which I am in prison—that I may make it clear, which is how I ought to speak. Walk in wisdom toward outsiders, making the best use of the time. Let your speech always be gracious, seasoned with salt, so that you may know how you ought to answer each person.
>
> Colossians 4:2–6

Here are five simple applications we can draw from this passage:

1. **Have the right mindset:** If you enter a conversation with a win-lose mentality, you've lost already. Our goal is not to

win a debate, but to open a door. Creative questions are one of the best ways to do that. "What do you believe? What has led you to care so much about this issue?"

2. **Speak your convictions clearly:** We're convinced God has revealed truth in his Word. In some ways, that removes the pressure—this isn't just our private hobbyhorse. It is what the Bible, God's Word, teaches.

3. **Pay attention to the conversational context:** Paul said we should "walk in wisdom." Wisdom is applied righteousness—knowing the right steps in the real world.

   • *Don't "yell in the library":* Are you at work, in a Bible study, on the street? These factors will determine just how the conversation proceeds.

   • *Discern whom you are speaking to:* Is he gay? Does she have an ideological ax to grind? Has he just learned his daughter is lesbian?

   • *Control the thermostat:* What is their emotional temperature (1 = calm; 10 = screaming mad)? If it starts to get hot, acknowledge it and take a step back. What is your emotional temperature? Wherever you are, keep cool. Otherwise, you give someone the right to write you off. Your conversation should be "gracious, seasoned with salt."

4. **Don't expect agreement every time:** In this passage, Paul basically asks God for the chance to say again, with clarity, what got him imprisoned in the first place! This isn't a popularity contest.

5. **Pray. Pray. Pray:** Enough said. Just pray. A lot.

My neighbors are a lesbian couple. We occasionally converse and have a cordial relationship. I've never out-and-out told them that I think their lifestyle is sinful. Am I just being a coward? Or is it okay not to mention this and just try to be a good neighbor to them?

1. **Be a good neighbor!** Build relationship. Be friendly, invite them to your home, go to their house, live some life with them. Don't be overly concerned with being the moral police. Let your Christian witness shine through your actions. This isn't being cowardly, it is just simple kindness. If I was your neighbor and the first thing you shared with me was your biblical worldview, I would think you're just weird. From my point of view, you can be more direct and honest the better friends you become.

2. **But don't be afraid of speaking the truth.** Seek opportunities to share the gospel of Jesus. The best way to do this is by sharing what Jesus has done for you. Don't make it academic; make it personal. This vulnerability is a non-threatening way to share the good news of Jesus. And when the time is right, don't be afraid to invite them to church.

3. **If things get heated, remind them that friends can disagree.** It is so silly that we have to walk on egg shells with those we don't agree with. If it is a real friendship, then there will be several areas of disagreement. This is okay. What is needed are respect, a listening ear, and a bit of humility.

4. **Become very aware of what God is doing in the life of this couple.** A good prayer to pray is this: "Lord, use me for what you want to do. Do you want me to serve them? Share biblical truth?" And then, as you are with them, seek to discern why God has you in a relationship with them. And as God opens doors, walk through them!

The bank where I work is celebrating "diversity week." The branch manager, whom I've been sharing the gospel with, is engaged in a homosexual relationship and has encouraged us

all to put a rainbow-flag magnet stating "Celebrate diversity!"
on our office doors for the week. What do I do?

First, don't display the rainbow-flag magnet. You may quail at
the thought. Your brain may cast about for a thousand reasons
to capitulate. "Maybe it will open up a door! Maybe I'll make
new friends! Maybe it will lead to my promotion, and then, as
a peer, I'll be able to share my convictions with my boss." These
reasons and more may rush through your mind.

Resist the urge.

Here's why: Because you do not support that flag. Since homosexuality is not God's plan for human flourishing, you know that
flag represents a declaration of independence from God's will.
That rebel flag is just another "stars and bars" of humanity's
civil war against God's kingdom.

Second, resist any effort to be drawn into a dead-end debate.
Simply maintain that you would "rather not" post the flag. If
asked, "Why?" reply that you "don't align with that particular
cause." When asked "Why?" humbly reply, "I value our friendship, respect your right to maintain your opinions, and ask that
you show me the same respect." Humble resistance is the key.

In Case of Emergency, Break Glass: If you begin to experience
negative treatment as a result of this stand, you should consult
your employee manual. While we don't advocate a litigation
frenzy, we do believe that Christians should be ready to guard
their individual rights. When we take a small stand for ourselves,
we're actually standing up for many others as well.

Let's be honest, in today's climate we are going to have a lot
of tests like this. We need to learn how to respectfully resist
budging. This is not a recalcitrant stubbornness or a desire to
oppress others. We do this because we still believe in the idea
of personal liberty and genuine tolerance (once greatly valued
in our country).

Our son is in a "dating" relationship with another man and wants to bring him home for the holidays. Should we allow this? What does this say to our family members? Would saying yes endorse their relationship?

First of all: your home, your rules. This is deeply personal; some parents just can't handle being around their kid's partner, and that is okay. Your son can't expect you to enter into his decisions and just accept them. To expect such blanket acceptance is just not reasonable. Your family life does not revolve around his choices. He needs to respect your boundaries and your moral choices. Instead, you can gently lay down a boundary: "We love you and would love for you, alone, to come home for the holidays."

Second, it would not be wrong to invite your son and his partner to your home for Christmas. Of course, they would stay in separate rooms. In loving ways you can be hospitable and honest. You can share the love of Christ and the gospel and show your son that you are for him even in his sin. Personally, this is what I (Ron) would do.

Finally, there are no easy answers here. What might be good for one family will not necessarily work for another. We need to make decisions slowly, prayerfully, and lovingly. Don't be reactive; do be willing to have hard conversations with your son. Why does he want to do this? Does he understand how painful this is for you? What is he feeling? Seek to love in the midst of turmoil.

The state where my gay brother lives just passed a marriage law, making it legal for same-sex couples to marry in the coming year. My brother and his partner are already talking about wedding plans. As a Christian, of course I don't agree with what they are doing, but if I refuse to go to this ceremony or if I speak out against it, I risk any sort of relationship with my brother and his partner in the future. What should I do?

This may be one of the most painful realities we will face in the coming years. If, as seems inevitable, the right to marry is universally extended to same-sex couples, then normally joyful announcements—engagements, showers, wedding invitations, adoption news—will become potential relationship bombs. As heartrending as we find it to give this answer, we advise believers *not* to attend a gay "wedding." The crux of the issue is summed up simply: We cannot celebrate what the Bible censors.

Weddings are a worshipful celebration of the God who made marriage. Marriage is not a man-made institution. It was designed by God as a source of joy for people and glory for himself. The marriage bond is not merely an emotional, relational connection between a husband and wife. It is an objective, spiritual reality created in heaven (Genesis 2:24; Matthew 19:3–9). Ultimately, human marriage is a creaturely analogue of Christ and the church.

When we attend weddings, we are joining with the assembled congregation and the host of heaven to say "Yes!" We are not only agreeing with the decision of two people to enter into a holy bond. We are agreeing with *marriage* as a God-ordained institution. We are agreeing with the God who designed the marriage bond. We are actually glorifying the God who seals two souls together.

But none of these things happen when two men or two women determine to call their relationship "marriage." Though they will it with all that is in them, their relationship is not marriage. It is, in fact, a thing that will destroy their souls if they insist on it (Romans 1:24–32; 1 Corinthians 6:9–10). The "wedding" that takes place is a celebration of something that deeply offends our

God. In a very real way, it is a worship service for a god of our own invention. How can we join such a God-dishonoring event?

We should not expect a gay family member or friend to understand these realities. From their perspective, our refusal to attend will be interpreted as a rejection of them. At some level, that feeling is inevitable. From their point of view, we are skipping out on a life-defining event. That is why it is important to communicate your love for them when you let them know that you are unable to attend.[1] It is also important to remember that God is absolutely capable of rebuilding this relationship and will honor your decision.

How can I start a conversation with a friend whom I believe may be struggling with homosexual feelings?

Interesting question. How do you know your friend is struggling? If it's his demeanor or just a gut feeling, I (Ron) would just build relationship, be kind, and be a gospel friend. I probably wouldn't ask. The hope is to build a relationship where your friend could be honest and share what is going on within. If he brings it to the friendship, it is much less intrusive than if you pry it out of him.

If he were to tell you that he was struggling with same-sex desire, then I would do four things:

1. **Make sure he knows how much God loves him** and that God has made a way forward through Christ. Same-sex struggle comes with deep shame. The good news of Jesus is that the cross cleanses us. Make sure your friend knows this.
2. **Make sure your friend knows that you don't think differently about him** because he has shared this. The truth is we all have our "stuff" that needs God's redemption.

You don't need to add to his shame by acting shocked or disgusted.

3. **Help your friend find help.** Ministries like Restored Hope Network (www.restoredhopenetwork.com) offer excellent resources and ministries that can help your friend navigate his same-sex desire.

4. **Make sure your friend finds a place to connect in your church.** He needs healthy community. Encourage him to find it. He might be afraid, but he needs this community if he is going to be successful in his discipleship.

What an honor to walk with someone with a same-sex struggle. Know that you are doing good gospel work as you help your friend encounter Jesus.

If my junior-high-age child persists in claiming to be a homosexual, should I discipline him? If so, how and to what degree?

I (Ron) am not sure what you mean by "discipline him." If your adolescent child is declaring his sexual orientation at such a young age, it is not a cause for discipline but for parental concern. You need to do a few things:

1. **Your child needs to know how much you love him.** Your love is unconditional. Reiterate it often, give hugs, and draw your son near.

2. **Why is he self-identifying as gay?** Seek to have non-threatening conversations where he can share what is going on in his life. Did he have a sexual encounter that caused him to question his sexual identity? Gently remind him that adolescents experience a variety of sexual feelings and most grow out of them and end up healthy heterosexuals.

3. **Get a wise pastor involved.** A good pastor might be able to help connect your son to the grace and mercy of Jesus. Your son, if he continues to have same-sex struggles, will have to navigate them as he seeks to follow Jesus. A good pastor can help him do this without shame.

4. **Seek a good Christian therapist.** If entering into this causes too much pain for the family or your son, it might be wise to consult a good therapist. There is one caveat: You must know that the therapist is a Christian who works within a Christian worldview and who believes that homosexual activity is sin. A good therapist can help the family navigate these difficult waters with grace.

5. **Your house, your rules.** As long as your son lives in your house, he must live under your rules. No gay relationships and no pornography in the house. You can help your son see that this is an issue of respect even if he doesn't agree with you.

6. **Pray.** The real hope here is that Jesus intervenes. I would fast, pray fervently, and ask the God of heaven to move on behalf of your son.

7. **Be hopeful.** God is in control. He will do good to your son. Believe! Watch. See!

I have a friend who is in a same-sex relationship. She says she wants to receive Jesus. Can she truly accept Jesus while she is still living this way?

An old hymn, often sung as the preacher pleads with people to come forward and pray the "Sinner's Prayer," intones, "Just as I am, without one plea, but that Thy blood was shed for me, and that Thou bidd'st me come to Thee, O Lamb of God, I come, I come!"[2] We all come to the foot of the cross just as we are. For some of us, the sin in our lives is buried deep below a surface appearance of moral uprightness and apparent success.

For others, it's blazoned on our chest like a scarlet A. But we all come sinful to the cross.

Though we might sin in different ways, we all come to the cross for the same reason. We have heard the gospel and believed it. We have seen our sin and want it no more. We have felt some trace of God's wrath and know we could never bear it. We have understood that Jesus, the perfect lamb, felt that wrath for us. And we now proclaim, "He died for me. I will live for him."

Can someone who is in a same-sex relationship be saved? Absolutely. However, that person will *absolutely* respond in obedience. She will understand that receiving Jesus as Savior means receiving him as Lord. True salvation is always accompanied by a transformed allegiance. Apart from that total surrender, we have no hope of true salvation.

Framing Your Own Response

We hope these practical responses will be helpful in your context. Even more, we pray that you will be able to grow in discernment, able to exercise biblical wisdom in real-life situations. As you seek to exercise compassion without compromise, we encourage you to keep two key principles in mind: mission and true love.

Mission—Jesus came to seek and to save lost people, and he has sent us out with that same mission.[3] We can *never* forget this. He did not call us to a "bumper sticker" mission, where we are content to advertise our convictions without ever entering into the sometimes messy world of relationships. When we are facing a tough choice, one essential question should be, "Will this help or hurt my call to witness in this person's life?"

True Love—The "true love" concept is at the heart of living out a life of compassion without compromise. In our day, people often act as if love and truth are at odds. Sometimes, people do live that way.

Let's face it. There are "truth" people, who dispense facts without any hint of love. Truth people are like guys who use a sledgehammer for every conceivable household task that includes hammering something. They might be trying to drive a stake into the ground to stabilize a sapling (good application), or a small nail into the wall to hang a picture (bad application). In the extreme, truth people do things like question the eternal salvation of a friend's grandmother while visiting the friend in the funeral home. Or respond to a gay co-worker's wedding invitation by saying, "God made Adam and Eve, not Adam and Steve." Truth people need to grow in true love.

Then there are "love" people, who refuse ever to speak a hard truth if they feel it might hurt someone's feelings. They are like an overindulgent, willfully blind parent who refuses to believe that "my little Johnny" would ever hurt another person, despite a track record of terrorizing his classmates, or like a doctor who would refuse to give someone a hard diagnosis if the treatment might inconvenience the patient.

A "true love" person understands that trying to sustain love without truth is like trying to breathe underwater. We are not showing *anyone* love when we encourage them to live out of touch with reality. At the same time, acknowledging the truth that it is potentially dangerous to dive below the surface does not prevent us from jumping in to save someone we love! Love drives us forward. Truth helps us chart a safe course toward the destination.

Ultimately, we believe it is important to understand ourselves, our strengths, and our weaknesses. Where are we tempted to compromise? Is it easier for us to shortchange love or to soft-pedal truth? A wise witness will understand these contours of their personality. They will want to stay balanced as they move forward in mission.

We won't pretend the answer is easy. Sometimes, the right call will only be known in eternity.

The Rest of the Questions . . .

Here are some more of the questions we received. Check out our online resources (www.CompassionWithoutCompromise. com) for answers to some of these questions.

1. **Can we just share the gospel without talking about the elephant in the room?**
   - Am I obligated to share my convictions with a family member who is in a same-sex relationship?
   - How do I respond to a gay friend whose only Christian interactions have been with "open and affirming" churches?
   - A gay couple I know asked me if my church would accept them if they came to church as a couple. How should I respond? My church maintains a biblical understanding of this issue—speaking the truth in love. Should I invite my friend and her partner to church? Would it seem like I'm trying to break them up?

2. **Can we have normal friendships without surrendering the truth?**
   - Should I stay in the home of a homosexual family member and their partner/spouse? Should I have them stay in my home? If so, should I have them share a room?
   - By attending a family member's same-sex wedding ceremony, could I open the door for future dialogue?
   - My sister is marrying her partner and asked my daughter to be the flower girl in the wedding. My sister and partner are both active parts of our family life. I know our church doesn't endorse homosexuality, so can we be

members of this church if my daughter is in the wedding as a flower girl?

- I have a same-gender co-worker who has become a good workplace friend. She recently began inviting me to connect (e.g., going to a movie, going downtown, or going to the mall). I've also become aware that she is an open lesbian. Should I hang out with this co-worker? I will be seeing her five days a week, eight hours a day for the foreseeable future. How do I show her Christ without turning her away?

3. How should we parent our kids in this new world?

- My teenage daughter (seventeen), who has shown increasing distance from the gospel, has announced to us that her friend of several years is now her "girlfriend." We've sought to call her back to Christ, but she is persisting in this and now argues that it is possible to be "gay *and* Christian." We love our daughter and are concerned for her, but we're also worried about the example she is giving to her younger brother and sisters. How do we proceed?

- My daughter tells me that her friend has secretly shared that she is homosexual. My daughter doesn't know if she can be friends with her anymore because it makes her uncomfortable. How do I affirm her convictions but encourage her to grow in compassion, avoiding hatred and bigotry?

- How do I explain to my kids in the age range of five to twelve what it means when someone "comes out" as gay or lesbian, helping them understand right, wrong, and God's plan for human sexuality?

- How do I explain my brother-in-law's same-sex wedding invitation to my ten-year-old?

- How much guidance should a parent have over their teenager?

- Should parents worry if their son is playing with dolls or is wearing girls' clothes? Should they worry if girls are too masculine?
- We have a same-sex couple in our neighborhood and they have two kids the same age as our kids. Our children play together, and now our kids have been invited to stay the night at the home of this couple. Should we allow this?
- Should I allow gay people in my life around my children, or would it give them a bad example of relationships?
- My son and his friends have developed a hateful attitude toward people at school who may be gay or lesbian. How can I help them see how their attitudes can have a terrible impact on their own hearts and on the lives of people who desperately need Jesus?

4. **How should we react to people and churches that claim Christ but support an open and affirming position toward homosexuals?**
   - If an actively gay person believes Jesus is the Son of God and risen from the dead, aren't they saved?
   - There are several places in Scripture that tell us not to have Christian fellowship with people who celebrate sin (2 John 10–11; 1 Corinthians 5:11; Matthew 18:17). Our churches are spineless when it comes to church discipline and not associating with those who persist in sin or false teaching. Yet I don't want to become so legalistic that we don't have fellowship with other believers who disagree about nonessentials of the faith. How do we know where to draw the line?
   - My Christian friend has chosen to become sexually involved with her female roommate. The community that surrounds them approves of their relationship, and some of them claim Christ. What is my responsibility regarding confronting those friends who both claim Christ and approve of the sexual relationship?

- Is it really possible to affirm gay marriage and retain the authority of Scripture?

- I have a relative who says that Paul would be fine with gay marriage because of 1 Corinthians 7:9: "But if they cannot exercise self-control, they should marry. For it is better to marry than to burn with passion."

- There is a lesbian couple coming to my church and they sit near our family. They act like a couple, hold hands, and see nothing wrong with it. How should I respond to them? What should I say to my children? Should our church allow this?

5. How do I maintain integrity in my workplace?

- I own a small printing business, and our non-Christian neighbor, who is actively involved in the gay rights movement, and with whom we've built a gospel-sharing relationship, has come to us asking our business to print flyers for the next local gay pride week. We think her intent, quite honestly, was to give us some business as an act of kindness. However, knowing her level of intensity on this, if we don't do it, not only will she be deeply upset, but she could take it to the state human rights council, which could fine us and push for the loss of our business license. How can we faithfully pursue a gospel witness and relationship with her?

- For many years I worked with a gay doctor. It was like the elephant in the room. My co-workers and I would share about things we would do or places we would go with our spouses, but we all really didn't want to know about her life. It made us uncomfortable. Was that fair? How do you work side by side with someone who is gay and still show God's love and compassion?

- I work at a Christian college where there is a clear Community Life Statement that prohibits acting out homosexual relationships. There are faculty members here who endorse and support homosexual behavior in the church. Is it my responsibility to confront those faculty members and pressure the leadership to remove them from the college?

- My stance on gay marriage seems to be the litmus test as to whether or not I should have a voice or platform of influence in our world. How do I make my stance clear without forsaking my right to speak?

- I have friends who run a photography business and have had to turn down a same-sex "wedding," and, in fact, are being threatened to shut down their business. Someone may wonder, "Why can't a Christian photograph a gay marriage?"

- What do I do if I book a client for my wedding business and only realize afterward that it is a gay couple's wedding?

6. Should my personal convictions be set aside at the ballot box?

- How do I respond when someone insists: "Though I believe in traditional marriage, I don't believe the government should legislate on personal choices like this. That's why I am voting 'no' to a constitutional amendment that would define marriage between a man and a woman. In the end, it's not hurting anyone else."

- My brother and his partner are very liberal politically and socially. They seem to despise all evangelical Christians because of what they hear from the more outspoken, finger-pointing televangelists. How do I overcome the stereotypical images people have of evangelical Christianity?

- Is there a difference between my civic responsibility and my Christian convictions when it comes to voting on gay-related issues? We live in a country that has historically made allowances for multiple points of view. Should

I vote based on my Christian convictions, or relegate those convictions to my own life and the life of my own congregation?

The truth is, it is going to take discernment to live faithfully in the new normal. No question-and answer-book will address each and every situation we face. However, by remembering the two values we mentioned—mission and true love—we believe that biblically committed Christians can be led into wise decision making. The good news is that we are not alone. In harmony with God's revealed Word, the Holy Spirit is present to lead us into authentic witness in a confused culture!

10

Don't Panic

Things might get hard,
but we're not alone.

Deer in the Headlights

Maybe you've watched it unfold: A Christian leader appears on one of those talking head "news" programs. The host, wanting to make his mark, shoots him a zinger. It goes something like this:

Host: So, Pastor Billy, can you explain why, in a world where dictators are torturing citizens, priests are molesting children, and terrorists are blowing up shopping malls, you feel the need to pick on gays? Are you really filled with hate or just shamelessly ignorant?

[Pastor Billy's eyes are wide-open caverns of terror. He thought he was here to discuss his new book Spiritual Growth for Dog Lovers—*about how different canine breeds each illustrate a fruit of the Spirit.]*

Pastor Billy: Umm . . .

Host: Are you still kicking your dog, or have you graduated to abusing your wife and kids?

[Against all laws of biology and physics, the pastor's eyes have widened. We expect them to drop out and onto the table at any moment.]

Pastor Billy: [sputtering profusely] I've never . . .

Host: Are you willing to issue a statement here and now that you have abandoned your message of hate, intolerance, and bigotry?

[An unmistakable look of relief washes over Billy's face. It appears he's been offered a reprieve.]

Pastor Billy: Yes!

Host: What do you say?

Pastor Billy: I'm sorry for anything I've ever said that has been hateful. Jesus loves everyone, and so do I.

Host: There you have it. Pastor Billy Bob Bolderson has repudiated his earlier statements on homosexuality. Pastor Billy, thanks for joining the rest of us in the twenty-first century.

This kind of programming leaves no option but the execution of a giant face palm. Watching it, we might feel a little twinge of "Better him than me!" Hopefully, any casual aspersions are mixed with a healthy dose of sympathy. We cannot really imagine having to stand up under that kind of pressure. Most of us will never have to.

That doesn't mean we are in the clear, though. The fact is we are all under pressure to conform to our world. This is a perennial struggle of the Christian life. It permeates the whole of our existence and presses down on us in ways we barely recognize. Increasingly, we will feel that pressure when it comes to homosexuality. Christians will be nudged toward open acceptance or submissive silence. We already feel this pressure in many circumstances. What can we do?

The "Gay Agenda"

For the last two decades, some Christian responses to homosexuality have resembled crazy people running around like beheaded chickens. We've been screaming and waving our arms, and acting like the world has never before faced such a crisis. It has.[1] In fact, the sexual mores of the New Testament world make twenty-first-century America seem somewhat tame by comparison (though we are quickly catching up).

In this panicked state, we have been tempted to view questions about homosexuality through the single lens of a big "gay agenda." In other words, we have dealt with this as a culture-war question, sometimes ignoring the real-world people who struggle with sexual identity issues. Yet these people—many of them open to the gospel—have been listening in on our sometimes overheated rhetoric. If we continue forward into the coming decade with this limited perspective, we're in trouble. Steadfast commitment to addressing homosexuality as little more than a political football or a front in the culture war will prevent us from building bridges for witness.

Most of this book has been aimed at encouraging us to view this issue through the lens of gospel ministry. The basic message of our deep guilt and God's amazing grace helps us see through the false dilemma that poses as unassailable truth: Either you affirm my lifestyle or you're hateful. The gospel frees us to stand beside our gay friends and point them to the cross that has saved and is healing us. It allows us to walk beside each other down a path of transformation that we all must travel—dying to self and rising again in Christ. Hopefully, you have found this approach helpful.

There Is an Agenda

While it is important to expand our vision beyond the culture-war template for addressing homosexuality, we should not be naïve. Even as we reach out with the gospel, we must be aware. The truth is, there is an agenda. There is a strong, organized movement across all levels of our culture. The aim of this movement is simple: To silence any opposition, not only to homosexuality, but to a wide range of sexual expression.

We are a long way from 1969, but many people point to this date and the Stonewall Riots as the bellwether of the gay rights movement. In the early morning hours of June 28, a police raid on a Greenwich Village gay bar at the Stonewall Inn ended with law enforcement being pushed back. Three days of rallies later, a new wave had taken shape. The gay rights movement had come crashing out of the closet, and America would never be the same.

The Gay Liberation Front was formed and took up the more radical tactics of the antiwar left. This original incarnation of the gay rights movement reached its apex in 1989, when protestors under the group name ACT UP stormed St. Patrick's Cathedral in New York City one Sunday during mass. These protestors were demonstrating against Cardinal John O'Connor, shouting slogans, carrying signs, throwing condoms, and crushing the consecrated wafer of the Lord's Supper into the floor. It was a public relations fiasco, and the movement viewed that moment as a setback.

In contrast to the more radical action of the GLF and ACT UP, other activists took a more measured, culturally savvy approach. Their strategy was outlined in what could be called the "public-relations bible" of the movement. This document was coauthored by two brilliant Harvard-educated thinkers, one a researcher in neuropsychiatry, the other an expert on public relations. Published in a magazine in 1987, originally called

"The Overhauling of Straight America," and later released in book form as *After the Ball*, this multi-step strategy reads like a historical retrospective of the gay rights movement penned in 2013.[2] It reframed the movement, pointing them away from the antiwar-style radicalism of the ACT UP crowd and toward a more public-friendly marketing approach.

Our goal here isn't to provide an extensive recounting of the gay rights movement. However, we believe it is impossible to live wisely in the here and now if we don't understand what got us here. Our contemporary attitude toward homosexuality is the result of a decades-long campaign. Over time, this campaign has built up steam. It is now a seemingly inexorable force. Key culture-creating organs—media/arts, education, and government—have been or have now become part of this campaign.

You probably don't need us to tell you this.

What you do need to hear is this: One of the key aspects of this campaign involves a turning of the tables. Essentially, once the LGBT agenda has gained sympathy (mission accomplished), then normalcy (mission accomplished), a critical component remains: to demonize those who are recalcitrant. To demolish remaining opposition.

In subtle and sometimes not-so-subtle ways, the weight of a movement with forty years' steam behind it is bearing down on those of us who are willing to love people but not tolerate falsehood. Our world has already begun to reprimand those who do not celebrate the LGBT message. Ironically cloaked in the sacred vestments of victimhood, a socially, politically, and economically powerful force is unleashing war on any form of opposition— whether it's an unwillingness to photograph a wedding or bake a cake,[3] a teenager's desire to overcome same-sex attraction through counseling,[4] or lifestyle standards for the leadership of a Christian college campus group.[5] Those who take such stands will be pressured by a force that feels nearly irresistible.

Don't Panic

At this point, your pulse may be pounding. You might be a little worried. Good. You should be. A little worried is okay. It means you have glimpsed the struggle that lies ahead.

If we were first-century Christians, we would talk about this struggle in epic terms. The book of Revelation depicts a great Beast rising from the ocean with many heads, horns, and crowns. It is ruthless, powerful, grotesque, and seemingly inexorable. Our twenty-first-century imaginations, emaciated by passive media consumption, have to work hard to get what John is communicating. In his vision, this great Beast is a satanic incarnation, a combination of demonic beings, political power, false worship, and socio-economic persecution. With great force, it bears down on the people of God, crushing them under the pressure of persecution. If John were drawing on our era's imagery, this Beast would probably be depicted as a kind of Vader-Sauron-Voldemort conglomeration of doom.

Through this powerful vision, John glimpses heaven's perspective on what the first-century churches are enduring, what the church has been enduring through the centuries, and what it will face in the days to come. John is peeling back the curtain on all things flesh and blood to reveal a deep spiritual battle that began in the garden of Eden and will conclude when God's throne descends to earth.

Reality check: We are a people who will face persecution until Jesus returns. To a world in open rebellion, we bring a message from the King. The world has never appreciated that announcement. Nevertheless, we have been given a job to do. In some ways, it seems like an almost impossible task.

On one hand, we have been called to Christlike compassion. We are being called to radically inclusive love. We hope you have felt challenged to love more freely. We hope all of us will gain a much deeper sympathy for those who are living with deep sexual brokenness or in blatant rebellion against the King. We hope that the doors of our hearts and our churches will swing wide open to our gay friends. May they be welcomed in to hear the gospel that saved sinners like us.

On the other hand, we have been called to an uncompromising Christlike courage. We are not allowed to budge. To give one inch on this means denying the gospel to those who need it most. Any *hint* of theological drift will disconnect us from the rock of Truth, setting us adrift into a "make it up as you go along" version of sexual ethics. The great theological debates in the past have often been tipped toward truth because a very few were unwilling to give any ground. That is where we must stand. *No compromise.*

We will need to be like a mother in the first contractions of labor to give birth. She knows that something painful, exhausting, and unavoidable is coming. It will test her, try her. All she can do is go through it. But something beautiful will greet her on the other side of that struggle. Something beautiful will be birthed in us and our churches on the other side of our struggle if we stick with it.

We will have gained a portion of Jesus' own compassion. As we truly befriend "the other" whose struggle seems so different from our own, we will discover what it meant for Jesus to walk beside broken people. Even more, we will discover how much we have been the objects of his love and compassion.

We also will have gained the honor of standing without compromise beside the Lord. There is a measure of Christlikeness that can only come when we suffer for it. Hear us clearly: We are not promoting some misguided form of medieval self-flagellation. That is the opposite of grace. At the same time, Scripture teaches something clearly: Jesus is very close to us when we are suffering for him.

This is the promise he made through John in Revelation to the churches as they faced the Beast. These churches were positioned in a pagan culture filled with idols and moral decay. They were constantly tempted to compromise, whether through a lack of love or a lack of courageous conviction. To these struggling churches, Jesus promises a reward for those who remain steadfast. To one, he promises "the morning star" (2:28). To another, the "hidden manna" (2:17). To yet another, he promises "white garments" and his name in the "book of life" (3:5). In each instance, Jesus is promising the same thing: his presence. He will be with us through the struggle and meet us on the other side when it's all over.

Don't panic. Whatever may be coming, Jesus has shown us the way. He's walked that cruciform path before us.

Humbly, he came down.

Compassionately, he called us to repentance.

Courageously, he faced his Father's Cross.

Victoriously, he rose again.

Now, he wants us to take up our cross so that the world may know that there is good news.

Takeaway

We can't be afraid to stand strong. In ways we have not yet experienced, Christians will be nudged toward silence on this issue. We already feel this pressure in some circumstances. We can walk forward in compassion without compromise, knowing that our Lord has blazed the trail and now walks with us.

Appendix

The Watershed

Throughout our book, we have been operating from a specific understanding of Scripture. Namely, we believe that the Bible is fully inspired by God. As God's own Word, the Bible is our highest authority. Additionally, since the Bible is God's own Word, everything it teaches is true. Practically speaking, the Bible has total trump-card power over every competing claim. This idea isn't new.

In the words of the Reformation-era *Belgic Confession,* Articles 3 and 5:

> We confess that this Word of God was not sent nor delivered "by human will," but that "men and women moved by the Holy Spirit spoke from God," as Peter says. . . .
>
> We receive all these books and these only as holy and canonical, for the regulating, founding, and establishing of our faith. And we believe without a doubt all things contained in them—not so much because the church receives and approves them as such but above all because the Holy Spirit testifies in our hearts that they are from God, and also because they prove

themselves to be from God. For even the blind themselves are able to see that the things predicted in them do happen.[1]

In the last century, a man named Francis Schaeffer helped many people understand the gospel. Through his writings, speeches, and countless personal conversations, he used his unique gifts to reach out to a world set adrift on the shoreless sea of secular humanism.

A short distance from where Schaeffer lived in the Swiss Alps, one can stand at a geological formation known as a watershed. Perched at this point on the mountains on a rainy day, you can stretch out your arms and, on one hand, touch moisture that will wind its way from streams, to rivers, to the warm tides of the Mediterranean Sea. On the other hand, you can feel the brush of raindrops that will eventually work their way into the frigid waters of the North Sea. In other words, a watershed is a dividing line.

We believe that our approach to the Bible is the great watershed issue of the Christian faith. Is the Bible God's revelation to humankind, or is the Bible a collection of people's thoughts about God? That is the question. If it is the latter, then we are under no obligation to order our lives around the teachings of Scripture. If the former, then the Bible is the most precious possession on earth—God's own perspective on life's ultimate issues.

We offer four reasons Christians should receive the Bible as God's inspired, perfect Word:

First, Jesus Treats the Bible This Way

In John 10:34–35, we read, "Jesus answered them,' . . . Scripture cannot be broken.'" "Cannot be broken" is actually one Greek word (*outhenai*). That one word indicates that nothing in the

Bible can be discarded or destroyed. Unlike every man-made thing, the Bible will never crumble and fade. It is perfect.

Second, This Is How the Bible Speaks of Itself

In 2 Timothy 3:16–17, Paul wrote:

> All Scripture is breathed out by God and profitable for teaching, for reproof, for correction, and for training in righteousness, that the man of God may be complete, equipped for every good work.

Notice a few important points: First, Paul says that "all Scripture is breathed out by God," or inspired. In other words, we can't pick and choose. The whole product is a gift from God. Second, Paul uses the word *Scripture,* in Greek, *graphe*—a written thing. This indicates that the writings themselves have primacy. The Bible doesn't "become" the Word of God as we read it, or simply "communicate" the Word as the Holy Spirit moves through it. The very writings themselves are divine speech. Third, Paul uses the phrase *breathed out.* This indicates that God himself is the cause of Scripture. He is the origin of the Word. Finally, Paul says that Scripture is "profitable." In other words, Scripture can do what it does because it is what it is. Because Scripture is God's Word, it can transform our lives!

A second example worth noting is 2 Peter 1:19–21:

> And we have the prophetic word more fully confirmed . . . knowing this first of all, that no prophecy of Scripture comes from someone's own interpretation. For no prophecy was ever produced by the will of man, but men spoke from God as they were carried along by the Holy Spirit.

Notice something important: According to Peter, God not only inspires the authors with his words, he guides them to record those words accurately, so that all the words of Scripture are God's own words.

Third, Believers Throughout the Centuries Have Affirmed This

We could give many examples. Here are two from the early church. Writing in the second century, Justin Martyr commented:

> Since I am entirely convinced that no Scripture contradicts another, I shall admit rather that I do not understand what is recorded, and shall strive to persuade those who imagine that the Scriptures are contradictory, to be rather of the same opinion as myself.[2]

In other words, because Justin Martyr was convinced that Scripture is God's Word, he knew it could never present inaccurate, contradictory information.

Augustine, considered the greatest theologian of the church, outside of Paul, affirmed:

> It seems to me that the most disastrous consequences must follow upon our believing that anything false is found in the sacred books. . . . For if you once admit into such a high sanctuary of authority one false statement . . . there will not be left a single sentence of these books which, if appearing to any one difficult in practice or hard to believe, may not by the same fatal rule be explained away.[3]

Fourth, Our Own Lives Confirm This

Scripture is self-authenticating. We believe that the Holy Spirit who inspired the Bible is at work in the life of every believer, confirming its truthfulness. Jesus said, "My sheep hear my voice"

(John 10:27). He promised to send his Holy Spirit to guide us into all truth (John 16:13). True believers, filled with the Holy Spirit, will want to believe God's Word. Just as the E strings in a piano will resonate with a perfectly sung E note, the "strings" of a believer's heart will resonate to the tune of God's Word.

Even more, when believers order their lives according to God's Word, we discover *true life*! The psalmist wrote: "The law of the LORD is perfect, reviving the soul; the testimony of the LORD is sure, making wise the simple" (Psalm 19:7). In other words, our lives are transformed and changed when we embrace the Bible as our final authority. This *deep*, heart-level transformation is one of the most convincing evidences that the Bible is what it claims to be: God's Word.

These are just a few examples of the many reasons we have to place our full confidence in the Bible as God's holy Word. We would encourage you to explore this for yourself. Specifically, we suggest you check out *Systematic Theology* by Wayne Grudem (chapters 2–8).

Acknowledgments

From Adam

First, I want to thank Ron for agreeing to work on this project. It has been a true joy and privilege to labor together. I thank the Lord for saving Ron and planting in him a courageous vulnerability. His cheerful communication of challenging truths calls me to be a better minister.

Thanks to the many people who submitted questions for chapter 9. The response was amazing, reminding us just why this topic is so timely. You certainly forced us to put on our thinking caps!

I especially thank the people who have helped develop and refine the message of this book over several years. It was conceived as a college campus lecture and grew because good people have given me opportunities to present it in various formats. Thanks to Barbara Yandell, Hope for the Nations, Tom Akers, the Borderlands community, Corinth Reformed Church, RCA Integrity, and Spartan Christian Fellowship. Many thanks to Kevin DeYoung and Ligon Duncan for encouraging me to write this book and Ryan Pazdur for helping me find a publisher. Special thanks to Ellen Chalifoux for your helpful suggestions and keen edits (any remaining clunkers are entirely ours!). And to Andy McGuire: I'll never forget hearing you articulate the concept of this book with total clarity. Thanks for helping it become a reality.

Finally, thank you to the two communities in which I minister every day. To my church family, Peace: Thank you for allowing the Barrs to live with you, labor in the kingdom, and grow in discipleship together. To my wife and sons: Jen, you have prayed, patiently waited, sacrificed; your confidence in this project has sustained me. Boys, you have asked many times, "Is it done?" I'm happy to say, "Yes, now it is." I love you.

From Ron

There are many people to thank. First, I am so thankful for Adam Barr; it has been such a great joy to work with him and to see the Lord work in this process. He is a godly man and he lives out what he teaches. Second, I am thankful for Faith Church, where I pastored for seven years. What an amazing community! Your love of the gospel and your willingness to live in the scandal of grace is beautiful. Next, I want to thank Calvary Church, where I am now senior pastor. Your love of the broken and your desire to be a hospital is what excites me about you. God has big things in store. I am also thankful for Andy McGuire and Bethany House. I think this book is important, and I am so grateful you all did too. Your support and wisdom were invaluable to me. Finally, I want to thank my wife, Amy. Apart from Jesus, you are the best thing in my life; our very crazy, kid-filled life is a demonstration of the goodness of God. I dearly love you; it gets better every day.

For Further Learning

In addition to this book, we offer a number of free online resources, including a small-group discussion guide, video resources, and other tools that can be used to lead a group or to learn more on your own. Check out these resources at www.CompassionWithoutCompromise.com.

We suggest deepening your understanding of this topic by investigating the following titles:

Sam Allberry. *Is God Anti-Gay? And Other Questions About Homosexuality, the Bible, and Same-Sex Attraction.* Purcellville, VA: The Good Book Company, 2013.

Rosaria Champagne Butterfield. *The Secret Thoughts of an Unlikely Convert: An English Professor's Journey into Christian Faith.* Pittsburgh, PA: Crown and Covenant Publications, 2012.

John Calvin. *Golden Booklet of the True Christian Life*, trans. Henry Van Andel. Grand Rapids, MI: Baker Books, 1952.

Christ on Campus Initiative. www.ChristonCampuscci.org.

Andrew Comiskey. *Strength in Weakness: Healing Sexual and Relational Brokenness.* Downers Grove, IL: InterVarsity Press, 2003.

Robert A. J. Gagnon. *The Bible and Homosexual Practice: Texts and Hermeneutics.* Nashville: Abingdon Press, 2001.

Sherif Girgis, Ryan T. Anderson, Robert P. George. *What Is Marriage? Man and Woman: A Defense.* New York: Encounter Books, 2012.

Peter Hubbard. *Love Into the Light: The Gospel, the Homosexual and the Church.* Greenville, SC: Ambassador International, 2013.

Leanne Payne. *The Healing Presence: Curing the Soul Through Union with Christ.* Grand Rapids, MI: Baker Books, 1995.

Mark A. Yarhouse, PsyD. *Homosexuality and the Christian: A Guide for Parents, Pastors, and Friends.* Minneapolis: Bethany House, 2010.

Notes

Chapter 2: Two-Faced

1. C. S. Lewis, *Mere Christianity* (New York: HarperCollins, 2001), 213.

2. Donald Miller, "The Campus Confession Booth," *Leadership Journal,* Summer 2005, www.christianitytoday.com/le/2005/summer/4.62.html.

3. Kevin DeYoung, *Taking God at His Word: Why the Bible is Knowable, Necessary, and Enough, and What That Means for You and Me* (Wheaton, IL: Crossway, 2014), 120.

4. Dallas Willard, *The Spirit of the Disciplines* (San Francisco: HarperSanFrancisco, 1990), 24.

5. C. S. Lewis, *Mere Christianity*, 167.

Chapter 3: Not the Same

1. "Sheer grace" is one of my favorite phrases in the Heidelberg Catechism. "The Heidelberg Catechism," Q&A 21, Reformed Church in America, www.rca.org/heidelbergcatechism.

2. Some of the best recent writing on this can be found in John Piper and Justin Taylor, eds., *Sex and the Supremacy of Christ* (Wheaton, IL: Crossway, 2005).

3. Ben Patterson, "The Goodness of Sex and the Glory of God" in Piper and Taylor, eds., *Sex and the Supremacy of Christ*, 58.

4. C. S. Lewis, *The Lion, the Witch and the Wardrobe* (New York: HarperCollins, 2013), 25.

5. Beautiful examples of this are Christopher Yuan and Sam Allberry, who have written books about their experience and commitment. Christopher Yuan, *Out of a Far Country* and Sam Allberry, *Is God Anti-Gay?* See "For Further Learning."

6. By no means am I saying that one can be in the throes of sexual darkness and expect his/her marriage to fix them. Instead, when one has purity, even though whispers of darkness remain, marriage can be a beautiful gift.

7. Piper and Taylor, eds., *Sex and the Supremacy of Christ,* 224.

8. Ibid., 231.

9. Here, I do not refer to those Christians who see themselves as gay and celibate for the sake of Christ. Instead, I am referring to those who believe active gay relationships are acceptable in a journey as a disciple of Jesus.

10. Piper and Taylor, eds., *Sex and the Supremacy of Christ*, 26.

11. We explore this more deeply in chapter 8, "Spots on the Leopard."

12. It is helpful to note that anyone, heterosexual or homosexual, can easily make sex an idol, the difference being that homosexuality is innately idolatrous and heterosexuality is innately good.

Chapter 4: Jesus Is My Homeboy

1. David G. Myers, *A Friendly Letter to Skeptics and Atheists* (San Francisco: Jossey-Bass/Wiley, 2008), 76. Note: That's like saying, out of the 30,000 nuclear bombs ever created by the U.S. Department of Defense, only two fell on Japan, so they must not be that significant. Technically accurate, but completely misleading!

2. Robert A. J. Gagnon, PhD, "Barack Obama's Disturbing Misreading of the Sermon on the Mount as Support for Homosexual Sex," Republicans for Family Values, October 23, 2008, http://republicansforfamilyvalues.com/2008/10/23/theology-expert-says-obama-grossly-distorts-scriptures-to-support-homosexual-cause/.

3. We want to emphasize that we *in no way* support people who would use these passages as a pretext for suggesting similar punishments be carried out today. We believe that this form of law, while founded on moral principles that continue, does not apply within the political structures that exist today. There was only one "Israel" that existed as a theocratic nation-state.

4. Revisionist interpreters call these the "clobber passages," but we think this is an uncharitable description of these scriptural passages. We are not hoping to "clobber" anyone with the Bible. We simply want to understand how God's Word outlines God's pattern for human flourishing.

5. Three more examples: In Luke 24, we read about two disciples trudging down the road to Emmaus, hearts heavy with fear and grief. According to the latest reports, their Messiah has been crucified and laid in a borrowed tomb. They don't recognize Jesus when he comes alongside them and joins in their conversation. As he begins to unfold Old Testament teaching and demonstrate that it *all* points to the Messiah's death and resurrection, their hearts start to burn. When the trio sits down to eat, the disciples' eyes are opened and they realize that the Son of God has been leading them through the Word of God the entire time—words he had inspired long before being rocked to sleep in a Bethlehem stable.

Later in the same chapter of Luke, the resurrected Christ appears to the disciples and says this:

> Then he said to them, "These are my words that I spoke to you while I was still with you, that everything written about me in the Law of Moses and the Prophets and the Psalms must be fulfilled." Then he opened their minds to understand the Scriptures, and said to them, "Thus it is written, that the Christ should suffer and on the third day rise from the dead, and

that repentance and forgiveness of sins should be proclaimed in his name to all nations, beginning from Jerusalem. You are witnesses of these things."
24:44-48

The phrase "the Law of Moses and the Prophets and the Psalms" is another way of saying "the entire Old Testament." Here, Jesus tells the disciples that the entire Old Testament was about him!

In John 5:37–47, Jesus makes a critical point to the Pharisees, who are rejecting him and his ministry: If you really believed the Old Testament (specifically, the writings of Moses), then you would believe in me:

> And *the Father who sent me has himself borne witness about me.* His voice you have never heard, his form you have never seen, and *you do not have his word* abiding in you, for you do not believe the one whom he has sent. *You search the Scriptures* because you think that in them you have eternal life; and it is *they that bear witness about me,* yet you refuse to come to me that you may have life. . . . There is one who accuses you: Moses, on whom you have set your hope. For *if you believed Moses, you would believe me; for he wrote of me.* But if you do not believe his writings, how will you believe my words? (emphasis added).

Here Jesus makes a stunning connection between the Old Testament and himself, demonstrating that true belief in the Old Testament will be demonstrated by belief in him, and that true understanding of him is made possible as we grasp the Old Testament revelation about him.

6. In some instances, we believe the Bible does allow for divorce.

7. Robert A. J. Gagnon, *The Bible and Homosexual Practice: Texts and Hermeneutics* (Nashville: Abingdon Press, 2001), 228.

8. We use the term *sacramental* here in its broadest possible sense—as a visible symbol of a spiritual grace. In a narrower sense, the Bible defines only two sacraments: baptism and the Lord's Supper. Though many things in creation point us to God's amazing grace, it is important to recognize baptism and Communion are uniquely ordained by God to communicate the grace of the good news to believers.

9. For a close study of the theme of meals and Jesus' ministry, see Craig L. Blomberg, *Contagious Holiness: Jesus' Meals With Sinners* (Wheaton, IL: Inter-Varsity Press Academic, 2005). Check out pp. 103–111 for more on the miracles of multiplying food.

10. New Testament scholar Craig Blomberg makes this point in his book *Contagious Holiness*: "The unifying theme that emerges . . . is one that may be called 'contagious holiness'. Jesus regularly associates with the various sorts of sinners on whom the most pious in his culture frowned, but his association is never an end in itself. Implicitly or explicitly, he is calling people to change their ways and follow him as their master. But unlike so many in his world (and unlike so many cultures throughout the history of the world), he does not assume that he will be defiled by associating with corrupt people. Rather, his purity can rub off on them and change them for the better. Cleanliness, he believes, is even more 'catching' than uncleanness; morality more influential than immorality" (128).

11. Jesus also makes clear the consequences for those who refuse to make him King: They will be rejected on judgment day. We might not like to hear this, but the clearest teachings about hell in all of Scripture come in the words Jesus spoke while

he was here on earth. Jesus did more than invite people to get a taste of life in his kingdom; he clearly outlined the realities for those who did not enter into it. For a small sample, check out Matthew 5:27–30; 25:41–46; Mark 9:42–49; John 5:19–29.

Chapter 5: Ban All Shrimp

1. Lisa Miller, "Religious Case for Gay Marriage," *Newsweek*, December 15, 2008, 30.

2. "You shall not wear cloth of wool and linen mixed together" (Deuteronomy 22:11); "You shall not eat . . . the pig" (Leviticus 11:4, 7); "Tell them to make tassels on the corners of their garments throughout their generations" (Numbers 15:38); "Everything in the waters that does not have fins and scales is detestable to you" (Leviticus 11:12).

3. An exception could be Leviticus 18:19, "You shall not approach a woman to uncover her nakedness while she is in her menstrual uncleanness." This prohibition is not referenced in the New Testament and appears to be directly connected to the concept of ceremonial uncleanness. Presumably, a man would contract the ceremonial uncleanness of a woman through sexual intimacy during her period. With these conditions in mind, many conservatives would contend that this prohibition is related to Jewish ceremonial law and no longer applicable.

4. Gagnon, *The Bible and Homosexual Practice*, 113. Gagnon's treatment of this subject is, hands down, the most important available. We rely on his scholarship in this section.

5. For example, see Galatians 2:15–16: "We ourselves are Jews by birth and not Gentile sinners; yet we know that a person is not justified by works of the law but through faith in Jesus Christ, so we also have believed in Christ Jesus, in order to be justified by faith in Christ and not by works of the law, because by works of the law no one will be justified."

6. For example, see 1 Timothy 1:8–11: "Now we know that the law is good, if one uses it lawfully, understanding this, that the law is not laid down for the just but for the lawless and disobedient, for the ungodly and sinners, for the unholy and profane, for those who strike their fathers and mothers, for murderers, the sexually immoral, men who practice homosexuality, enslavers, liars, perjurers, and whatever else is contrary to sound doctrine, in accordance with the gospel of the glory of the blessed God with which I have been entrusted."

7. Well before Jesus was born, Jewish scholars had translated the Old Testament from Hebrew into Greek. Most of the New Testament authors, who wrote in Greek, made frequent use of this translation, called the *Septuagint*. We are often able to make important connections between the Old and New Testaments by seeing how the New Testament authors quoted and alluded to words and phrases from the *Septuagint*.

8. Gagnon, *The Bible and Homosexual Practice*, 312ff.

9. While it goes well beyond the scope of this book to develop this point, it is important to note that the New Testament clearly distinguishes church and state authority. For example, see Jesus' comments in Matthew 22:21 and Paul's in Romans 13:1–7.

10. Martti Nissinen, *Homoeroticism in the Biblical World* (Minneapolis: Augsburg Fortress, 1998), 109–112, quoted in Robert Gagnon, "How Bad Is Homosexual Practice According to Scripture and Does Scripture's Indictment Apply to Committed Homosexual Unions?" www.robgagnon.net/articles/HomosexHowBadIsIt.pdf.

11. Louis Crompton, *Homosexuality and Civilization* (Cambridge, MA: Harvard University Press, 2003), 114, quoted in Robert Gagnon, "How Bad is Homosexual Practice According to Scripture and Does Scripture's Indictment Apply to Committed Homosexual Unions?" www.robgagnon.net/articles/HomosexHowBadIsIt.pdf.

Chapter 6: Perception and Reality

1. David Kinnaman, *unChristian: What a New Generation Really Thinks about Christianity . . . and Why It Matters* (Grand Rapids, MI: Baker Books, 2012), 92–93.

2. Ibid., 93.

3. Leon Morris, *The Gospel According to St. Luke* (Grand Rapids, MI: Eerdmans, 1974), 189.

4. "Lesbian, Gay, Bisexual and Transgender Health," Center for Disease Control and Prevention, www.cdc.gov/lgbthealth/youth.htm.

5. John Calvin, *Golden Booklet of the True Christian Life,* trans. Henry Van Andel (Grand Rapids, MI: Baker Books, 1952), 37.

Chapter 7: Here's the Church, Here's the Steeple

1. "Historic Earthquakes: 1964 Great Alaska Earthquake," *U.S. Geological Survey,* http://earthquake.usgs.gov/earthquakes/states/events/1964_03_28.php.

2. We recommend picking up Allberry's book *Is God Anti-Gay?*

3. You can learn more about the GSA Network here: www.gsanetwork.org.

Chapter 8: Spots on the Leopard

1. Restored Hope Network, "Mission Statement," www.restoredhopenetwork.com.

2. See the following article from Aaron Blake: "Christie signs bill that bans gay conversion therapy," *Washington Post,* August 19, 2013, www.washingtonpost.com/blogs/post-politics/wp/2013/08/19/christie-will-sign-bill-that-bans-gay-conversion-therapy. We should expect that such stories will multiply in the years to come.

3. Mark Yarhouse, *Homosexuality and the Christian* (Minneapolis: Bethany House, 2010), 41.

4. Ibid.

5. Ibid., 42.

6. C. S. Lewis, *Mere Christianity* (New York: HarperCollins, 2001), 215.

7. Augustine, *The Confessions*, trans. Maria Boulding (New York: New City Press, 1997), Book IX, 177–178. Augustine famously confessed his own desire to postpone discipleship so he could continue indulging his lusts.

8. Sam Storms, *One Thing* (Scotland: Christian Focus Publications, 2004), 18.

9. John Calvin, *Golden Booklet of the True Christian Life,* trans. Henry Van Andel (Grand Rapids, MI: Baker Books, 1952), 27.

10. Ibid., 29.

11. Dietrich Bonhoeffer, *Life Together: The Classic Exploration of Faith in Community* (New York: HarperCollins, 1954), 118–119.

12. For more information about either ministry, visit www.desertstream.org or www.celebraterecovery.com.

Chapter 9: When Push Comes to Shove

1. For a great response from Pastor John Piper, check out this audio: "Would You Attend a Gay Wedding?" Desiring God Foundation, October 10, 2013, www.desiringgod.org/interviews/would-you-attend-a-gay-wedding.

2. Charlotte Elliott, "Just As I Am," 1835, public domain.

3. See Luke 19:1–10 and 24:44–49.

Chapter 10: Don't Panic

1. Imagine ministering in a world where a man would shack up with his stepmom. Prostitution, drunkenness, and orgies were central to the *worship* of many cultures. An entire line of pottery in the ancient world was built around grown men giving gifts to boys they were molesting (*kalos* pottery).

2. Some dispute the claim that this book provided a "blueprint" for all factions in the gay rights movement, but it is impossible to deny that it certainly laid out a game plan that seemed to be executed with precision over the next two decades.

3. Sterling Beard, "NM Supreme Court Finds Refusing to Photograph Gay Wedding Illegal," *National Review*, August 22, 2013, www.nationalreview.com/corner/356498/nm-supreme-court-finds-refusing-photograph-gay-wedding-illegal-sterling-beard; Liz Fields, "Judge Orders Colorado Bakery to Cater for Same-Sex Weddings," ABC News, December 7, 2013, http://abcnews.go.com/US/judge-orders-colorado-bakery-cater-sex-weddings/story?id=21136505.

4. Ian Lovett, "Law Banning 'Gay Cure' Is Upheld in California" *New York Times*, August 29, 2013, www.nytimes.com/2013/08/30/us/law-banning-gay-cure-is-upheld-in-california.html?_r=0.

5. InterVarsity outlines the legal challenges it has faced on its website here: "Campus Challenges," *Intervarsity*, www.intervarsity.org/page/campus-challenges.

Appendix: The Watershed

1. *Belgic Confession,* Articles 3 and 5, www.crcna.org/welcome/beliefs/confessions/belgic-confession.

2. Justin Martyr (2nd century), *Dialogue with Trypho,* quoted in John Woodbridge, *Biblical Authority: A Critique of the Rogers/McKim Proposal* (Grand Rapids, MI: Zondervan, 1982), 32.

3. Augustine (4th century), letter to Jerome, quoted in Woodbridge, *Biblical Authority*, 37.

Adam T. Barr (MDiv, Western Theological Seminary, ThM, Trinity Evangelical Divinity School) serves as senior pastor at Peace Church in Middleville, Michigan. In addition to his work in the local church, Adam launched and leads Borderlands, a ministry that fosters next generation leadership development, and served on the board of RCA Integrity, a renewal movement in the Reformed Church in America. Adam lives with his wife, Jennifer, and four sons in Middleville, Michigan.

Ron Citlau (MDiv, Western Theological Seminary) serves as the senior pastor of Calvary Church near Chicago. Ron helped produce curriculum on sexual healing now used by Desert Stream Ministries in hundreds of churches throughout the country. Ron lives with his wife, Amy, in Crown Point, Indiana.

Get More Out of
COMPASSION *without* COMPROMISE!

Whether you are reading this book on your own or as part of a group study, be sure to take advantage of the bonus material available on the *Compassion Without Compromise* website. Here, authors Adam T. Barr and Ron Citlau provide a study guide to facilitate deeper reflection and discussion, ten chapter introduction videos, shareable downloads, key quotes, and more.

CompassionWithoutCompromise.com